LEAVES FROM ROWAN'S LOGS

St. Joseph's College of Education,

WITHDRAWN FROM STOCK

Cruises on West Coast
of Scotland

by

DR. R. B. CARSLAW

Second Impression

Frontispiece : LOCH TORRIDON

ROBERT ROSS & CO. LTD.

(*Sole Distributors :* ROLLS HOUSE PUBLISHING CO., LTD.)

ROLLS HOUSE, 2 BREAMS BUILDINGS

LONDON, E.C.4

Made and Printed by
Sydenham & Co. (Est. 1840) Ltd., Oxford Road, Bournemouth

PREFACE

Vessels large may venture more,
But little boats should keep near shore.

MY wife and I realizing with reluctance that our cruising days are done have been consoling ourselves by re-reading our logs, by looking again at our sketches and photos and enjoying in retrospect the pleasures of wandering up the West Coast of Scotland.

Wishing to share this enjoyment with our family I decided to collect extracts from these logs and some of the sketches and photos, and thus remind them of the happy times we had had with them.

Knowing that there are many who enjoy reading about cruising among the islands of Scotland and elsewhere I have ventured to publish these leaves from our logs in book form. I hope that sailing men will enjoy reading them, and that others after accompanying us on our wanderings will become infected with the joys of life afloat and be encouraged to go and do likewise.

This, then, is the story of how a young family were allowed to hear the call of the sea, and of how their parents enjoyed watching them answering it.

At first the youngsters had to be shown how to fly, but after they had learned to use their wings and had left the nest they had the audacity to come back and try to evict their parents. Many of the entries, especially in Part I, may seem trivial, even childish, but several of the family were then mere children, and this is a record of family sailing.

No apology is due for the countless references to weather forecasts, gale warnings and rainfall, as for these the vagaries of our climate are responsible. With the exception of occasional really fine spells we had, during these twelve years, poor weather and more than our share of gales.

PREFACE

The detailed description of the yachts may appeal to some readers more than to others, and the same applies to the notes on the navigation of unfrequented anchorages and the numerous references to depths, tidal streams, direction and strength of the wind. All soundings are those at L.W.O.S. (Low Water Ordinary Spring Tides) except when otherwise stated, and the Beaufort scale is used when referring to the strength of the wind.

As we had four boats this book must have four parts, each representing a stage in the family's development, and I have tried in sorting out this bundle of leaves to avoid monotonous repetition.

The water colours are by my wife : the photos were taken by various members of the family. Several of the latter have already appeared in the *Yachtsman*, and one in the *Yachting Monthly*.

To K. Adlard Coles I am greatly indebted for criticism, advice and encouragement.

R.B.C.

Dunrowan, RHU, DUMBARTONSHIRE,
1944.

NOTE.—The spelling of place names in this book is based on that adopted in Admiralty charts and the *Clyde Cruising Club Journal*.

CONTENTS

ILLUSTRATIONS

ILLUSTRATIONS

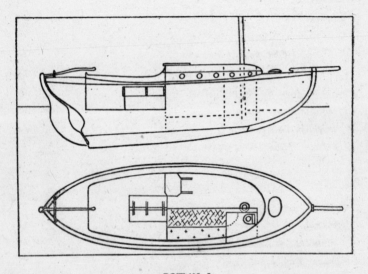

ROWAN I

L.O.A. 27ft. 6ins.   L.W.L. 23ft. 6ins.   Beam 8ft.   Draft 3ft. 9ins.

LEAVES *from* ROWAN'S LOGS

* * *

PART I

The Leaves are Green — 1927 to 1928

Rowan I. A CENTRE-BOARD SLOOP

BEING fortunate in having a house at Rhu, at the mouth
of the Gareloch, while still in practice as a surgeon in
Glasgow I bought a small yacht in 1927 with the object
of accustoming my young family to the difficulties and discom-
forts, the problems and pleasures of sailing, hoping later on
to have a boat big enough and a crew experienced enough to
take us all up the West Coast.

The yacht was a six-ton centre-plate sloop, built by McGruers
of Clynder for a Marine Exhibition in Glasgow in 1926. She
was 27 ft. 6 in. *length overall*, 23 ft. 6 in. *length water line*,
with 8 ft. *beam* and 3 ft. 9 in. *draft* ; Bermudian rigged with
417 square feet *sail area*, and with a 7/9 h.p. Thornycroft
Handybilly as auxiliary.

Her accommodation consisted of a fo'c'sle with a pipe
cot and a Primus stove ; a cabin with almost 5 ft. headroom,
off which there was a compartment with a w.c., and a large
cockpit in the middle of which was the engine casing.

We called her *Rowan* and the 9-ft. round-sterned dinghy
was dubbed *Bud*.

The family consisted of Neill, John, Mary, Bob, Charlie,
my wife and myself, our ages at that time being respectively
5, 7, 12, 15, 17, 46 and 48.

11

In the summers of 1927 and 1928 we spent all our spare time afloat mostly in day-sailing, but with many short cruises to Loch Goil, Loch Long, Millport, Loch Ranza, Tarbert Loch Fyne, Loch Gair, Loch Riddon and the Kyles of Bute.

The two older boys soon became handy with the sails, although there were occasions when I was glad there was no gaff to endanger the heads of the younger ones. The yacht was inclined to be tender so we became after a few trials quite expert at reefing, but because of this tenderness and her slowness in getting to windward in a short sea the centre-plate was removed and a lead keel added in spring, 1928. This greatly improved her windward work, and incidentally gave us more room in the cabin.

We carried all manner of stores and as space was very limited stowage of movable articles below was one of our problems. (" On our way home from Hunter's Quay we got a heavy squall which upset everything below, but not my wife's equanimity : lunch A.I.") Although our cooking facilities were limited never was food more highly appreciated. When sailing we usually had our meals in the cockpit, but at anchor as many of us as could crowded into the cabin.

As a rule only three slept on board, the others finding what accommodation they could ashore. But even before the centre-plate casing was removed we could squeeze in four as the following note of a night at Loch Riddon proves : " A lovely evening with phosphorescence, star-fish and bagpipes ; poor Mary having dropped her spectacles overboard in Rothesay Bay, (they were ' not really lost as we know where they are ' !) with her right eye bandaged and her right hand also after an encounter with a tin of peaches, was in great form in the fo'c'sle cot ; Bob a bit cramped on the floor, but Charlie and I snoring contentedly on the settees."

Mary's log tells of an interesting night she and my wife spent in a cottage at Colintraive. As etymology was not part of *Rowan's* curriculum, I am not responsible for the somewhat unusual spelling.

" Dad, Mummy, Charley and myself went for a cruise in *Rowan* on tuesday for two days. We went by engine to the Clogh lighthouse ; we put up the sail then and we saild to Rothsay bay where we took in a reif because it was prety windy there. We had to tack up the cyles. Charley took Mummy

and me ashore at Colontrive, and we walked along the road to
see if we could get a room for us to sleep in that night. It
was now about 7 o'clock, and we went aboard and had dinner.
A little while after dinner we all went ashore and Dad and
Mummy went to the hotel to see someone (I wonder why !),
Charley, Bob and I waited outside. Then we went to our
room and Dad and the boys went to the yaute.

" In the middle of the night I wakened up and found that
Mummy had been downstairs, and also that a little babby
girl had been born. In the morning I saw the little babby,
then we had breakfast and went aboard. We went up Loch
riden to Ormedail and then through the cyles to Towered
lighthouse by engine. Dad switched the engine of, a light
breese sprang up and we saild to Roaseneath Patch. The
we put on the engine and mottered home as we were in a hurry."

We do not agree with surly Dr. Johnson that " a ship is
worse than a gaol ; there is in a gaol better air, better company,
better conveniency of every kind, and a ship has the additional
disadvantage of being in danger."

But of course young people must be kept busy, especially
if herded together as we were. With a little help, chiefly
from my wife, they kept themselves occupied each in his or
her own way. Charlie had charge of the engine and spent a
lot of time trying to get a most inefficient wireless set to function.
Bob was more interested in deck work and navigation. John
and Neill spent hours in the dinghy taking soundings, and on
board, when not being read to by my wife, played countless
games of draughts. Mary, when not engrossed in a book,
collected specimens for an aquarium. She also did a little,
a very little, knitting. In my log is a short entry referring to
a woollen garment which was being made for the " babby "
at Colintraive. " Mary knitted 3 rows : 123 stitches, 123
heavy sighs."

So we kept them busy and happy and very seldom were
there any squalls although it is rather significant that on one
occasion I wrote in the log that " we spent a most enjoyable and
peaceful day; I was busy on board, all the others were ashore."

By autumn 1928 we felt able and experienced enough to
handle a larger boat and so get rid of the trouble of finding
sleeping quarters for some of the crew ashore. So *Rowan*
was sold and McGruers were asked to build her successor.

PART II

In Full Blossom — 1929 to 1934

I

Rowan II. A Bermudian Ketch

THE problem Ewing McGruer was asked to solve was to design a boat with a moderate, easily-handled rig, with dry decks and stability rather than speed, with comfort below and sleeping accommodation for seven, and with a deck-house which would not spoil the general appearance of the craft. He was restricted as to tonnage as I was not prepared to tackle an anchor of more than about 70 lbs. and the crew might often be reduced to only three.

He met these conflicting requirements by giving us a light displacement 11-tonner of 37 ft. 6 in. *length overall*, 28 ft. *length water line*, with 9 ft. 8 in. *beam* and 5 ft. *draft*;

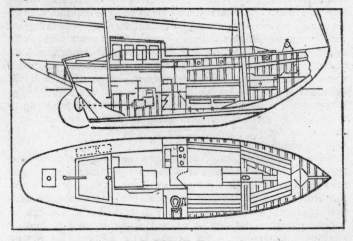

ROWAN II
L.O.A. 37ft. 6ins.   L.W.L. 28ft.   Beam 9ft.   Draft 5ft.   Tonnage T.M. 11 tons.

14

Bermudian ketch-rigged with 577 sq. ft. *sail area*, 6-ft. headroom, and with a 7/9 h.p. Thornycroft Handybilly as auxiliary.

For various reasons *Rowan II* was not ready till July so we had to give up any idea of " going north " this year. This was probably fortunate as we had to find out any weak points, appreciate the good ones and generally make friends with the new ship.

So we contented ourselves with many short cruises inside Cantyre, and in addition to re-visiting our 1927 and 1928 anchorages found several new ones. We did not care for Lamlash ; it was too big and too sophisticated. In Black Harbour, on the east side of Loch Fyne opposite Tarbert, we found a secluded spot which appealed to all of us. We lay at the head of the bay close to a small jetty, but had we been there in a strong southerly we might not have been too happy, as it is somewhat exposed. Our favourite anchorages were Swine's Hole (a small bay south of Carrick Castle, Loch Goil) ; Wood Farm Buoy, well out of the tide inside the buoy at the east end of the south passage in the Kyles of Bute ; Loch Riddon, just off the wreck on the shore opposite Ormidale ; and, of course, Tarbert, Loch Fyne, in spite of its soft smelly mud.

We soon became more confident and more skilled in finding the best spot, and we had no trouble in handling the 72-lb. Fisherman's *anchor* and 50 fathoms $\frac{3}{8}$-in. chain. The double-acting ratchet lever winch made work easy, and the chain stowed itself without any attention into a locker in the fo'c'sle. We dragged twice : at Swine's Hole it was due to a " foul anchor " ; at Tarbert it was caused by a westerly gale which got up during the night. We were almost ashore at 6 a.m. but shifted just in time in a deluge of rain with the help of the Handybilly. In less than half an hour we had re-anchored and with the added assistance of a 26-lb. " angel " stayed put ; but some of us *were* wet.

But I have been putting the cart before the horse by describing anchorages before we have set sail.

As the *mainsail* had only 346 sq. ft. we had no difficulty in handling it ; roller-reefing was new to us, but as we had lots of hard winds we soon appreciated its advantages. The *mizzen* was disappointing, as under it and the jib she made a poor showing on the wind even when it was blowing hard. *Steering* was by tiller or by wheel, but as none of us liked steering from the deckhouse even when under power the wheel was scrapped later.

Thanks to stanchions and a double *life-line* we had little fear of " child overboard," but I confess to finding myself every now and then hurriedly counting the ship's company to make sure that all were there. Although we could have carried the dinghy on deck I preferred to tow it, especially when there were children on board. We frequently, without any preliminary warning, carried out " practice life-saving " by heaving a cork stool overboard, abandoning the tiller and leaving it to the younger members of the crew to retrieve it as quickly as possible. They could, of course, all swim ; John passed our second highest test this year by jumping overboard and swimming round the ship. (Neill followed suit in 1931 at Totaig.)

The *Handybilly* was installed under the deckhouse floor and was readily accessible. It gave us six knots in quiet water and the fuel consumption was only $\frac{3}{4}$ gall. per hour. It was not powerful enough to drive us against a strong wind and sea, but it was intended to be merely an auxiliary.

The *deckhouse* was a prominent feature, too prominent according to some of my critical friends who called it the " conservatory " or " tramcar." Any drawback, however, was more than compensated for by the advantage it was, especially to the young folk. In wet weather, and we had plenty of that, the whole ship's company could congregate there, and many were the games played and the stories read in its shelter. At anchor, also, one could see what was going on without having to jump up and look through a port-light every time someone saw something passing somewhere. Outboard from the settee on starboard was a most useful locker for crockery and in large lockers on port there was ample room for all sorts of domestic stores.

The *cockpit*, which was approximately 5 ft. × 4 ft., was well sheltered by the deckhouse. It was supposed to be self-emptying by means of two drain pipes, but if we were heeled it was more inclined to be self-filling. It had a grating of which we were at first very proud, but which proved to be a nuisance as all sorts of stuff collected under it. As it was difficult to lift out I had it divided, but even so we got very tired of trying to keep it bright and clean.

The *fuel tanks* (10-gall. paraffin, 4-gall. petrol) were housed on the port side and had readily accessible turn-off cocks. A pyrene fire extinguisher was kept near the engine and another in the fo'c'sle.

A Vortex centrifugal *pump*, which had a truly remarkable delivery rate and could tackle anything from matches to bits of wool, was rarely used.

There was fully 6 ft. headroom below decks, thanks to the high freeboard. Underneath the two built-in bunks in the fo'c'sle there were roomy lockers for all sorts of gear and forward of the bunks was the sail locker.

In the *cabin* the port settee and back (which hinged up) made fairly comfortable berths, but our pride was the 6 ft. × 3 ft. built-in bunk on starboard. It had a V-spring mattress and lockers below with sliding doors and was for my wife. She also had a wardrobe at its forward end recessed into the fo'c'sle, in a corner of which we kept a small wireless set.

Aft of the cabin there was on starboard a *lavatory* (where we hung the oil-skins), and a *galley* on port. This latter, in which was a two-burner " Clyde Cooker," was much used as the appetites of the crew seemed to increase out of all proportion to the advance in their ages. My wife was naturally the chief performer here but Charlie often lent a hand. *Water*, of which we carried twenty-five gallons in a tank under the cockpit floor, was drawn by a hand-pump to the galley, where there was also a supply of fresh drinking water in a three-gallon " stock pot."

A second-hand dynamo which we installed was run by a belt off the flywheel and gave us electric light everywhere.

I must not forget the eighth member of the crew, " Billy," a faithful Aberdonian. He was quite happy on board but enjoyed himself most when ashore chasing rabbits who had at least twice his speed and whom he never caught. His morning run ashore was a good excuse for getting the young ones out of their sleeping bags. On one occasion he was an unmitigated nuisance. Having lain overnight at Blackfarland Bay, Bute, we were anxious to get off early, but when taken ashore " Billy " quietly made off. We searched in vain for him for hours on the shore and up the hill, and only when we had given up in despair did we discover him hiding within a few yards of the dinghy.

It might be supposed, and it was often said, that by trying to get a lot into a little we were too overcrowded and cramped, but that was not the case. Thanks to our experience in *Rowan I* and to Ewing McGruer's ingenuity we now had a boat which while no flier was stiff, dry, easily handled and with all the comfort that could be desired.

I have described in considerable detail the equipment and arrangements of *Rowan II* as such matters are of interest to cruising men. Those readers who may have skipped impatiently over them will, I hope, have become infected with the joys of life afloat after accompanying us on our wanderings. Thirsting for an explanation of how one can live in comfort and safety in a small boat they will drink in all the details of *Rowan III* and asking for more will get another instalment with *Rowan IV*.

Rowan I
Off Loch Goil

Rowan II
Off Tarbert, Loch Fyne

Bud AND *Berry* RACING IN RHU BAY

LAUNCH OF *Rowan II*

CREW IN *Rowan I* : NEILL, JOHN, MARY, BOB, "BILLY," CHARLES, MY WIFE

The Road to the Isles, Looking North from Crinan

The Basin, Crinan

II

Four Cruises up the West Coast

FULL of confidence in our new ship—and her crew— I now felt justified in taking them further afield, and in each of these four years we had a cruise of about a month " up north."

As a mere repetition of our logs would be wearisome, and as many of our anchorages were frequently re-visited, I will combine the four cruises in *Rowan II* in an omnibus narrative following the coast and not the calendar. This will include a description of several passages in addition to notes of personal incidents and of places and things of general interest, but I must be careful lest it take the form of a Cook's conducted tour complete with guide.

Before embarking on this composite cruise, in which the chronological sequence of events is necessarily rather confused, I will give a list of our anchorages in each, and thus remind my crew and allow any interested reader to follow each cruise. A few remarks about the weather we experienced and any alterations, improvements or precautions which we found necessary when fitting out will also not be out of place.

* * *

1930.

When fitting out we found that we had neglected to take a lot of necessary precautions when laying up and the result had been seized or rusted gipsy of winch, cocks of w.c., pump, tanks, etc.

A large reaching jib was bought which we hoped to use on occasion as a spinnaker.

Bud was converted into a first-class sailing dinghy by a dagger which McGruers fitted and a lugsail which we made ourselves. This added not only to the enjoyment of the crew (and the anxiety of the skipper !) but also to their experience in handling a boat under sail.

After a few preliminary cruises to make sure that everything was shipshape, we, seven all told, plus " Billy," left Rhu on July 4th, hoping to get as far north as possible in three weeks and to return still seven all told, plus " Billy."

Our anchorages were :

Rothesay ; Tarbert, Loch Fyne ; Ardrishaig ; Crinan ; Puillodobhrain (two nights) ; Dunstaffnage ; Loch Drumbuy (2) ; Loch Aline ; Puillodobhrain ; Macnevan Island, Loch Craignish (3) ; Tayvallich, Loch Swen ; Gigha ; Campbeltown (3) ; Wood Farm Buoy, Kyles of Bute and home on July 25th.

We had not got far north, but our passage round the Mull of Cantyre in a No. 8 gale had put the finishing touch to the confidence we had in our ship. Not only had we made friends with her, but she had found herself. Apart from this gale we had experienced moderate winds.

After our return we had a short cruise with *Fiara* in Loch Fyne, and then re-visited our favourite Clyde anchorages before laying up at the end of August.

1931.

As the result of a generous use of grease when laying up we found everything more satisfactory when fitting out this year.

The only change we made was in the engine fuel ; we gave up paraffin and used only petrol. The reason for this was that we had so often forgotten to switch over from paraffin to petrol before stopping with the result that the carburettor had to be cleaned out. As this was not noticed until we had tried unsuccessfully to start it was apt to lead to loss of time and temper. We considered that our precautions—tank-fillers on deck, accessible turn-off cocks, pyrene in fo'c'sle as well as deckhouse—eliminated any risk of a serious fire. In fact we felt safer than before because with a leakage paraffin might lie unsuspected in the bilges.

A few more pigs of lead were added to the internal ballast, bringing it up to 16 cwt. This with the iron keel gave us a total of 3 tons 14 cwt. ballast.

To allow us to have some dinghy racing in Rhu Bay I bought a second 9-ft. centre-plate dinghy which we called *Berry*. As she was square-sterned and could carry all of us more comfortably, she displaced *Bud* on this year's cruise.

After three short cruises in the Clyde we got away from Rhu on June 27th with five weeks at our disposal, with all the crew on board and flying now the Royal Cruising Club's burgee.

Our anchorages were :

Wood Farm Buoy; Tarbert; Crinan; Loch Spelve; Loch Aline (3); Loch Drumbuy (2); Canna; Loch Scathvaig; Isle Ornsay; Totaig, Loch Duich (4); Acarsaid Mor, South Rona; Totaig; Eigg; Loch Drumbuy (2); Loch Aline; Dunstaffnage; Puillodobhrain (4); Craobh, Loch Shuna; Tayvallich (5); Isle Righ, Loch Craignish; Tarbert, and home on August 2nd.

Although we were disappointed at having to return via the Crinan Canal owing to our mishaps when making for Gigha, we were quite pleased to have got as far as we did. We had had very treacherous un-summerlike weather, although on only three days were there gale warnings. We were all sorry that we had missed *Fiara* and resolved that we would not do so next year.

1932.

Apart from some trouble with the three-way cock and exhaust pipe fitting out was fairly normal. The method of cooling the exhaust by turning the circulating water into it has given us more bother than our forgetfulness about switching over from paraffin to petrol. The carburettor could fairly easily be cleared of paraffin, but when water left in the exhaust pipe gets back into the cylinders it is a much lengthier and dirtier job getting rid of it. The " snifter valve " which is supposed to prevent this was most unreliable. The only way to avoid trouble is by not forgetting the three-way cock, or better still by having a water-jacketed exhaust pipe. (See *Rowan III* and *Rowan IV*.)

We now had a double topping lift, and ordinary reefing gear in addition to the roller reefing which had let us down last year.

After our usual preliminary short cruises we left Rhu on June 25th with five or six weeks in hand. We were already beginning to have some trouble collecting our full crew. At Ardrishaig Charlie had to return to his work, rejoining ten days later at Tobormory. A friend, Miss C., temporarily took the place of Mary whom we were to pick up at Oban. " Billy " had unfortunately died last autumn, but " Jack," another Aberdonian, took his place.

LEAVES FROM ROWAN'S LOGS

Our anchorages were :

Colintraive; Ardrishaig; Craobh; Puillodobhrain; Dunstaffnage (3); South Shian, Loch Creran (3); Port Ramsay, Lismore; Loch Aline; Tobormory; Loch Drumbuy; Charna, Loch Sunart (2); Loch na Beist; Plockton, Loch Carron; Badachro, Gairloch; Dunvegan (2); Canna (2); Tobormory (2); Bailachloidh Harbour, Gometra; Bunessan, Loch Lathaich; Erraid, Ross of Mull; Brandy Stone, Oban; Dunstaffnage; Shuna Cove, Loch Linnhe; Puillodobhrain; Fearnoch, Loch Melfort; Isle Righ; Tarbert and home on July 31st.

We had on the whole better weather this year. There were only two days with gale warnings, but we had lots of wind. This cruise was made all the more enjoyable by our good fortune in meeting and sailing with *Gigha, Morna* and *Fiara.*

1933.

When fitting out this year we resolved, we vowed, that all tanks, filters, fuel pipes and carburettor must be emptied and cleaned out when laying up. While Charlie had the unpleasant job of clearing out all the " muck," and attending to other mechanical tasks, I spent some days laying teak floors throughout the ship.

The Clyde Cooker was the worse for wear—and no wonder, it had been much used—so we substituted for it a " Latham." This, with its 2-gall. copper fuel tank, pump, pressure gauge, filter and 2-level supply tap was a decided improvement.

I left Rhu on June 24th in a downpour of rain with an unusual crew : Bob and other four medical students. The four left at Ardfern when the rest of the family arrived with the exception of Charlie, who did not join us till July 15th at Tobormory.

Our anchorages were :

Colintraive; Tarbert; Ardfern, Loch Craignish; Isle Righ; Ardfern; Puillodobhrain; Brandy Stone; Dunstaffnage (2); Kintallen, Loch Linnhe; Camus na Gall, Lochaber; Port-an-Dun (2); Loch Aline; Tobormory (2); Loch Drumbuy; Salen, Loch Sunart (2); Tobormory (2); Mallaig; Totaig; Acarsaid Mor, South Rona; Kenmore, Loch Torridon; Shieldaig, Loch Torridon; Portree; Loch na Beist; Tobormory; Oronsay, Loch Sunart; Loch Drumbuy; Eil. Garbh, Loch Sunart; Salen, Loch Sunart; Puillodobhrain; Isle Righ; Colintraive and home on July 30th.

We had much quieter weather during this five weeks' cruise, and were also fortunate in having the company of *Blue Dragon* and *Fiara.*

26

III

Coastwise : Gareloch to Loch Leven

AFTER these necessary preliminary notes I now come to the narrative of our wanderings up the West Coast. Having some idea beforehand when all or most of the crew would be available I took care to have all the gear and unperishable stores on board in good time. We usually set off " all of a sudden," and just as we were impatient to get to Crinan and beyond as soon as possible, so I am unwilling to waste time and space describing our passages to Ardrishaig. Leaving Rhu sometimes late in the day and having, up to 1933, to " lock in " at Ardrishaig within three hours of H.W., we usually anchored for the night at Colintraive or Tarbert on the way.

Crinan Canal.

If we got in before midday we went straight through ; if not we had to lie in the Basin at Ardrishaig and, in spite of the attraction of the eels and the opportunity of buying stores we had forgotten to bring, we did not relish this.

Naturally during our first passage through the canal, with its fifteen locks and four swing bridges, there were moments of anxiety. Unfortunately we had to share the locks with another yacht and had little room to spare. We saved ourselves a lot of trouble by carrying the dinghy on deck, and we had no mishaps except when " Billy " fell into a lock, to be quickly rescued none the worse by Mary. We found, after our first passage, that we could manage quite well without a man, but " the exhibition of rope-throwing by my wife, Mary and even Charlie, came in for much well-deserved criticism."

Notwithstanding the friendliness and interest of the Canal staff at Crinan, we were as little inclined to linger there as at Ardrishaig. The thrill when the first time we emerged from the high-walled sea lock and set out on " The Road to the Isles," was perhaps not so intense on later occasions, but it was always there.

The beauty and attractions of this nine-mile stretch of inland water-way were appreciated even more on our homeward passages. There was peace and calm after perhaps a " stoory " time outside ; the banks were covered with flowers, and many wildfowl could be seen swimming ahead and hiding in the reeds. But there was a feeling of sadness and regret as we could not help wondering if we would all be back again next year.

Loch Craignish.

As soon as we were clear of the lock we were so busy tidying up the mess on deck, stowing warps, fenders, etc., that we had hardly time to look at the fine old castle of Duntroon standing out prominently on the north shore of Loch Crinan. When the tide at the Dorus Mor (setting through at 6 to 8 knots Springs, and making 1¼ hours before H.W. and L.W.) was not favourable and the " Great Door " was thus closed, we went up Loch Craignish for the night.

Passing Rabbit I. on starboard and Port nan Lion on port, we were soon at the Black Rock on which dozens of seals were lying. Only when we got almost near enough to photograph them did they slide clumsily into the water, their heads re-appearing soon after close astern.

On our first visit (in 1930) we slipped in between More I. and Macnevan I and found a land-locked anchorage in three fathoms. One drawback, and it was a sticky one, was the very muddy shore. When waiting there for weather suitable for a passage home round the Mull of Cantyre, the Crinan Canal being closed, we made an expedition to Kilmartin walking the long eight miles there, but thankful to get a local bus back. In the churchyard at Kilmartin there are many old sculptured stones, and in the glebe four large cairns covering " cists " or burial chambers of great archeological interest (see page 110).

In 1933 we found our way round the north end of Macnevan I. passing another Black Rock, and anchored between Iscan Isle and the small stone pier. This quiet Ardfern anchorage has many advantages ; it is beside a local bus route and a telephone ; there is an occasional provision van, a water supply and perfect shelter in from two to four fathoms.

Another good anchorage in this loch is on the east side of Righ I. just below the farm. To get three fathoms one has to

go well inshore, and by doing so is sheltered from both north and south. We had been here in 1931 and 1932 and I came back again in 1933 with the young medical students. They were indeed a cheery lot. Six of us set off in the 9-ft. dinghy at 10 p.m. with a splash net, and we must have rowed over ten miles before returning at 2.45 a.m. with two sea trout and a lobster. We lost three trout which fell out of the net, and another, the best one of course, which one of the crew dropped overboard when admiring it. After a short but profane silence we nearly lost him in the same way ! We had " supper," including the lobster, at 3.15 a.m. and turned in when dawn was breaking—to sleep and not to dream. As the medicals were due to board MacBrayne's bus at the cross-roads two miles from Ardfern at 10.15 a.m. we were not long in our bunks.

We came back to this anchorage again a month later with *Fiara* on our way home. Some of both crews went ashore to inspect the ruin at Old Poltalloch. We had been told that the owner had been so devoted to his Irish wife that he had had the garden filled with soil brought from Ireland. Another perhaps more likely explanation was that the boats which took potatoes to Ireland during a famine there had returned with earth as ballast. The shore party intended walking " over the hills and far away " to Kilmartin, but they found the hills too far away and got nowhere.

From 11 p.m. till nearly 2 a.m. Bob and I " splashed," and as we caught only two sea trout we left the net out all night. In the morning we had quite a big catch—two mackerel, half-a-dozen dog fish, hundreds of crabs, thousands of jelly fish and tons of seaweed. Surely this will cure us of illegal fishing. (But it did not.)

Loch Craignish to Puillodobhrain.

When on our way north we left Loch Craignish in time to catch the first of the flood through the Dorus Mor so as to carry it up past Fladda. In 1930 having passed Craignish Point we took the passage between the shore and Ris an Vic Faden and, giving the north end of the island a clear berth, ran to the red buoy off Ardluing Point. We were still carrying a strong flood when we passed Fladda, keeping mid-channel to avoid the foul Luing shore and the 6-ft. rock north of N.

Fullah. With a rising wind we passed close to the fine Seil cliffs, scarred with trap-dykes, and rounded Ardencaple Point. As there was now driving mist we stowed our sails and motored into Puillodobhrain, keeping clear of the rocks at the north end of Eil. Dun.

In the following year after leaving the Dorus Mor we took the outer passage, between Ris an Tru and Vic Faden, taking good care to avoid the nasty 2-ft. rock off Corr-easar. We knew that if the light southerly failed, there was some danger of being drawn into Coirebhreacain, but we had the Handybilly to fall back on if necessary. The wind softened, but although we could hear the roar in the Gulf we were able to hold our course up Scarba Sound. My wife was the only one who showed any anxiety, but she had an excuse for this. Some years before a large cutter in which she was cruising was drawn in, and she remembered the anxiety shown by the Captain and crew before they got safely through after many involuntary gyrations.

There is some doubt as to the meaning of the word Coire-bhreacain. Some hold that it should be translated as the Cauldron of the Speckled Sea. The explanation given by Martin in his *Description of the Western Islands*, seems sounder. He writes : " This gulf hath its name from Brekan, said to be son to the King of Denmark who was drowned here, cast ashore, on the north of Jura and buried in a cave as appears from the stone, tomb and altar there."

Puillodobhrain.

This " Pool of the Otter " became one of our favourite anchorages and only in 1931 did we pass it on our way north. We looked into Easdale once, but finding little enough room there, resumed our journey to Puillodobhrain after a few hours. On our way south we invariably paid it a visit. On entering for the first time we wisely used the engine, but after we got to know the rather narrow channel, we made a point of sailing in unless there was a head wind. One may anchor anywhere, in three faths., but the best spot is just inside the entrance opposite the trap-dyke on port, where one is sheltered even from a N.E. gale (see page 169). In the evening G. I. Taylor,

---

who was lying near us in *Frolic* (R.C.C.) paid us a visit and after inspecting the ship and her crew offered to put me up for the Royal Cruising Club. We were greatly flattered and accepted the offer with thanks.

This was an ideal place for the young people. Although there were only a few low islands between us and the wide Atlantic the " lagoon " was so land-locked that we could safely allow them to sail in the dinghy and wander as they cared about the islands. But in spite of the quietness I find from my log that John fell out of his bed (above me) at 1 a.m. ; he apologized in the morning for having disturbed me and when asked how it had happened, said, " I wakened to find myself falling through space ; I couldn't make out where I was, before I found out I had gone to sleep again "; as I found him sound asleep on the cabin floor I covered him up and left him.

Unfortunately there is no good water supply here, only a somewhat brackish pool on the north side of the trap-dyke. So next day we, all seven of us, went down Clachan Sound under sail in *Berry* to get water at the hotel at the bridge. We discovered that the south-going ebb starts 1¾ hours before H.W. only when we were struggling back with the oars. This " Bridge across the Atlantic " was completed in 1793 from plans by the famous Telford ; it has a single arch with about 25 ft. above H.W. Although at one time it was used by boats plying between Oban and Crinan, and " vessels of forty tons burthen could pass through the channel with big tides," it has silted up largely owing to debris from the slate quarries at its north end. There is now a bar there which dries at low water, and it is navigable only towards high water for motor boats of light draft. It was at Tighnatruish Hotel, the " house of the trousers," that the inhabitants of Seil used to change their garb before going south in the days when the wearing of the kilt was forbidden.

Below the bridge the sound opens out into a small bay with three fathoms, where a boat could lie safely all the year round. From here to Balvicar Bay in Seil Sound the channel is narrow and tortuous, but there is a least depth of 1½ fathoms at high water.

There is great natural beauty in this intricate collection of mainland and islands, of land-locked bays and channels, of ever-changing tides, where all manner of wild fowl may be seen. A short scramble up the hillside gives one a wonderfully extensive view, to the north the Firth of Lorn as far as Lismore; to the south, Scarba, Jura, and on a clear day Colonsay and Islay; while to the west, past the south coast of Mull with its high cliffs, one looks out to the Atlantic itself.

As the nearest store is at Balvicar, about two miles from the bridge, we usually preferred to go on and get what we needed at Oban.

Oban

Oban has been called the Charing Cross of the Highlands as from here steamers sail to all the ports in the west. But so far as yachting people are concerned this is not an apt description as nobody uses it as a terminus. Everyone comes here to go somewhere else.

As there is no comfortable anchorage in the bay we followed the usual custom by anchoring at the Brandy Stone, but even here it is difficult to get less than eight fathoms. The holding, however, is very good and it is surprisingly sheltered.

But having got all the stores we require we will push on and in my omnibus narrative of our four cruises in *Rowan II* we will follow the coast and not the calendar.

Dunstaffnage

Leaving Oban Bay, usually well after lunch, if the wind was westerly we slipped round to Dunstaffnage and, as at Puillodobhrain, we used the engine when entering for the first time. At our subsequent visits, and they were many, with a favourable wind we would run in under sail, and, even though there was usually not a breath of wind as soon as we had passed the point, would carry enough way to reach the anchorage. The bay dries out for a long way but one can get from five to seven fathoms off the jetty well out of the tide.

On our first visit " my wife, Mary, John and Neill ashore almost before the anchor was down; ashore again after tea seeing the Castle; ashore again after dinner seeing the dungeons thanks to the kindness of the caretaker's wife who had been a nurse in a Glasgow nursing home." That was the usual

Footnote: In 1940 I took a small feu on the hillside to the east of the bridge hoping soon to have a house built there and to be able to moor *Rowan IV* in this bay in winter and at Puillodobhrain in summer, but Hitler's refusal to admit that he is beaten is rather spoiling our plans.

routine : all except Bob and perhaps Charlie would make for the shore as soon as possible, but it allowed me to get everything stowed in peace. In the evening, we made friends with *Deirdre* (Webster and Naismith).

The Castle is in ruins : it originally belonged to the MacDougalls of Lorn, was taken over by the Crown, and then in 1436 given to the Campbells. Lying in a corner are some guns removed from the Spanish galleon *Florida* sunk in Tobormory Bay. In the wood near the Castle is the ruin of a small chapel, a beautiful example of early Gothic architecture. But the historical interest of this place goes much further back as from the sixth to the ninth century it was the seat of the Court of the Pictish and Scottish Kings. The Lia Fail, or Stone of Destiny, which was brought about A.D. 500 from Ireland by Fergus Mor, who founded the Kingdom of Dalriada, remained here until its removal to Scone. It was later, in 1296, removed by Edward I to Westminster Abbey, where it still is in spite of the efforts of the Scottish Nationalists.

When we were lying here for several days in 1932 because of strong winds much of the time was spent on the sand at Grouse Bay, just over the point, where most of the crew found the bathing excellent. But when *Morna* (R.C.C.) belonging to Robert Workman, a cousin of my wife's, came in under mizzen and jib with the owner and other Irish friends on board, we deserted the sand and sat in *Morna's* cabin eating sweets, drinking lemonade, etc. and talking till a " wee short hour ayont the twal'."

South Shian, Loch Creran

As *Morna* wished to go to Loch Creran we decided to accompany her there and to continue up Loch Linnhe after she had turned for home (Cultra, Belfast). Although Dunstaffnage Bay was quiet there was quite a big sea outside, and the southerly was still strong, so we hoisted only mizzen and jib. With this we ran up the Lynn of Lorn to the entrance of Loch Creran, and at half flood, using Chart 2814A (Loch Linnhe, southern part) easily identified the " dries 10-feet " and " dries 6-feet " rocks off Rudha ard Beith. The line Branra Rock showing north of Eil. Glas was very useful when keeping clear of the string of rocks off the north-west of Eriska. We anchored in six fathoms just inside the line between South Shian Ferry and the farm on Eriska, putting down twenty-five fathoms and an angel as it was looking very black to the south. *Morna* came in later and anchored far out in a downpour of very heavy rain.

Next day, after *Morna* had left under reefed main and mizzen, we rowed across to North Shian, crossed in the ferry from Port Appin to Lismore, had a look at Port Ramsay, and when returning had a perilous row with wind and tide to South Shian.

Port Ramsay, Lismore

Beating out next morning with the last of the ebb we narrowly missed a rock on port before we had reached those marked on the chart and decided that the line of rocks shown there should extend further north-east. Passing between Eil. Glas and the " dries 10-feet " rock, we bore away up channel to Grey I. and then beat back to Port Ramsay. Dropping the mainsail we found our way in cautiously, but without real difficulty, as the " dries 10-feet " rock was easily picked up. We found a snug anchorage inside Eil. nain Meann in five fathoms, well-sheltered except perhaps from the north. In various " sailing directions " one is told to anchor as soon as the ruin on the west shore shows over a dip on the islet, but to see the ruin *over* the islet one would have to climb the mast, and a tall one at that. The proof o' the pudding is the preein' o' it !

Shuna Cove, Loch Linnhe

Later in this year (1932) on our way home from Iona, having sailed round both Skye and Mull, after laying in stores at Oban we were on the point of leaving for Puillodobhrain when to our delight *Fiara* appeared, motoring up the sound from the south. Mutual jubilation and visitations. I was evidently showing signs of relief after our somewhat venturesome wanderings, especially as I felt that I would now have the support of McStay in curbing my reckless crew, for I find this entry in the log : " The skipper, his worries being now over, slept continuously for ten hours. Mary said that she had not known that there had been any occasion for worry at any time." Thank you, Mary !

We lay that night at Brandy Stone, and after a day at Dunstaffnage carried a fine southerly up the Lynn of Lorn to Shuna Sound. As there is depth enough in the south passage only at high water we came in round the north of the island and found a good berth, sheltered even from the north, in five fathoms between Knap Point and Shuna Isle just below the sheep fank.

Some of us walked to the farm for milk and eggs and found that the farmer and his wife had supplied us with similar necessaries two years ago at Loch Craignish. It was a most beautiful afternoon and evening after a wet windy morning. In the evening we all visited Castle Stalker, a square conspicuous tower which stands on a small island at the mouth of Loch Laithaich. It is said to have been built for the use of James IV during his hunting expeditions in the neighbourhood, hence perhaps its name.

Kintallen, Loch Linnhe

In 1933 we sailed from Dunstaffnage to Kintallen, where we had difficulty in finding less than seven fathoms. While Bob and John climbed a hill (Charlie was not with us then !) I walked past Lettermore Point and had a fine view of Glencoe. After dinner we bought a 6-lb. grilse from a fisherman who was lifting his nets. Although this is a beautiful bay I would not care to lie here in northerly winds, but salmon straight from the sea are certainly an attraction.

Camus na Gall, Lochaber

Leaving Kintallen with a light south-westerly, we passed through Corran Narrows with the flood and, the wind freshening, were soon anchored at Camus na Gall. The best spot is in three fathoms off the fence to the north of the ferry-house with the south point of the bay just shutting in the railway pier at Fort William. We had seen *Blue Dragon III* lying off Fort William and were delighted when she came across and anchored beside us with the owner (the late) C. C. Lynam on board.

We spent the evening with Lynam, and although his ship was unspeakably untidy below decks, he and his crew, three young maidens and two young men from Oxford, were as happy as could be. Lyman when signing my copy of *The Log of the Blue Dragon*, told me that I was lucky to have got it, even secondhand, as he had recently tried in vain !

Although my mind may have been at ease in these quiet waters, my natural irritability was evidently unabated as I remember being very annoyed when Mary insisted on deserting us for a day. We put her ashore at Corpach, and from there she went by rail to visit a friend at Spean Bridge, returning late in the evening by ferry from Fort William. I could understand the pleasure it gave the young people to go ashore, but to desert the ship for a whole day seemed to me quite outrageous !

Port an Dun, Loch Leven

With *Blue Dragon III* we left Camus na Gall, under power as there was not a breath of wind, intending to get the first of the flood through the Peter Straits into Loch Leven. As usual we were far too early, so shutting off the engine at Corran Narrows, we hoisted all sail and got through against the last of the ebb without touching, although we got into one and a quarter fathoms off the south point. We then hauled out of the current into Port an Dun and, seeing the rock in mid-channel awash, ran between it and the rocky promontory on port, anchoring off the Bishop's House in three fathoms.

" It was hot, hot, very hot to-day ; much bathing by everybody in the afternoon ; when we turned in at 11 p.m. the sky was very thundery looking."

Early next morning there was heavy rain and strong squalls from all quarters. Just as we were sitting down to a shockingly late breakfast in the deckhouse I realized that we were dragging. So the table was hurriedly cleared and the engine started, but we had actually pushed off the rock with the spinnaker boom before we had the anchor up and shifted into the inner bay. The reason we had dragged was that we had during the night been pirouetting round our anchor in the squalls and, the chain having got completely tangled up with the stock, we were riding to five fathoms in five fathoms. (It is impossible to avoid this risk with a Fisherman, but for the cure of the trouble see our cruises from 1935 onwards.)

In the afternoon we rowed against a fresh easterly to St. Mungo Island to see the ruined chapel and burial ground. I noted that " the island was disappointing ; a lot of gravestones and nettles and no water." We had a look at the anchorage which some recommend to the east of the island, but agreed that it would offer little shelter from north-east to south-east, and would be exposed to heavy squalls from the Glencoe mountains. Both when going and coming back we had to put all except Bob and myself ashore to make rowing possible except when actually crossing to the island. " A very fine day of great heat and strong wind."

Blue Dragon III, who had been at Kinlochleven, came in in the evening and Bob and Mary joined her crew (less the owner) in a hill climb and did not get back till midnight. As it began to blow hard I slipped down an angel, but Lynam, refusing our offer of help, shifted anchorage single-handed under power.

The wind took off during the night, and after a late breakfast and a good weather forecast we ran through the Peter Straits with the ebb and, passing the mouth of Loch Corrie, entered the Sound of Mull.

ST. MUNGO ISLAND. See photograph, page 57

IV

Sound of Mull to Sunart

Loch Spelve

AS on our return from the North we usually made direct for Puillodobhrain, I will refer to Loch Spelve before leaving the Firth of Lorn for the Sound of Mull. It was at my wife's suggestion that we explored this loch in 1931, the only time we by-passed Puillodobhrain on our way north. Entering one and a half hours before high water, we got in safely with the help of Chart No. 2813 (Lochs Buy and Spelve, Mull) and Charlie's keen eyesight, and anchored in five fathoms behind Amleig I., where *Blue Dragon* had ridden out a gale on New Year's Eve in 1899.

Next day with a falling glass and pouring rain we were not patient enough to wait for the flood, but picking up the four leading marks, two of which we had failed to find the previous day, we got out without touching. With a good southerly we then had a fine run under full sail to the Sound of Mull, until we lost the wind at Grey Rocks. After drifting about for a while we were hit by a sudden squall from the north, and there was some confusion below deck, the only damage, however, being a broken tea-pot. With a rising north-westerly, we then beat into Loch Aline. We had a somewhat similar experience two years later when, after only light airs at Ru Redire, we got very strong squalls off the Morven cliffs and had to drop the mainsail. A curious place this and worth watching.

Duart Castle, a striking feature standing out so prominently above the point, can hardly be passed without comment. After lying in ruins for a long time it was restored by the combined efforts of the clan, and in 1912 the Chief, Sir Fitzroy MacLean, came back to live there. There was a great gathering of the clan on his hundredth birthday in 1934, although by that time he was very feeble and died soon afterwards.

A Maclean of Duart, one of his ancestors, being for some reason annoyed at his wife, a sister of the Earl of Argyll, marooned her in 1530 on Lady Rock off the south end of

OPPOSITE : CAMUS NA GALL, LOCH LINNHE
DUART CASTLE. See photograph, page 58.

Lismore. Whether the rising tide would have drowned or merely scared her depends on the time of year that he chose, as the rock covers only at equinoctial Springs. However, she was rescued by some of her brother's men with the result that there was a feud between the clans and MacLean met his death a few years later by the hands of another brother.

Loch Aline

One point about the entrance to this beautiful loch is worth noting. The two white concrete posts inside the narrows on port give a line to clear Bolorkle Point and not, as is generally supposed, the course through. One should keep mid-channel until well past the stone pier and then, as the loch opens up round Kyle Point, carry on to starboard and anchor east of the Point in five or six fathoms.

On our first visit we had very strong winds for two days, first from the north and then from the south with heavy rain. We rowed across to the store, but got neither papers nor a tea-pot; we walked to the old churchyard at Kiel and saw the old grave-stones which are carefully preserved in the ruined church; we walked to the ruined castle at Ardtornish Point, one of the strongholds of The Lord of the Isles; and when in the evening the rain cleared " it was warm with perfect odour of cut hay, honeysuckle and meadow sweet, with a perfect sunset in a mackerel sky." There are indeed compensations for the vagaries of the West Highland climate.

The young people were greatly intrigued by seeing a rabbit which they had disturbed swimming across a pool at the foot of a waterfall on the east side of the loch. But what interested my wife most were the lias fossils. These date back to the Jurassic period, when extensive areas of Europe were invaded by the sea. There were myriads of these fossil shells on the shore and their presence embedded in the rocks high up on the cliffs showed very strikingly how high the water had at one time been.

Tobormory

Our next port of call was of course Tobormory. Sometimes we beat up the Sound against the prevailing north-west wind, but we preferred to wait for a fair wind. I was usually allowed to make this short passage without interruption, but once was persuaded, or should I say ordered, to anchor for a few hours in Salen Bay to allow some of the crew to see the ruined Aros

Castle. There is a small bay to the north of the Castle which would give good shelter except from the east. The shore party arrived back with a bouquet of flowers, a gift from the gardener, as a solatium, but I did not appreciate this as flowers are a nuisance in a small boat.

During these four years we were often in Tobormory, sometimes waiting for weather favourable for the passage round Ardnamurchan, twice to pick up Charlie who was coming by MacBrayne's steamer, but more often to get letters and stores, including " Old Mull " a very good brand.

We came across all manner of boats there, many of them were small hardy cruisers like *Grace*, *Morag*, *Monica* and *Elspeth*. In 1931 we were very pleased to meet an old family friend, R. Bruce Taylor. A retired Professor of Theology in Canada, he showed no signs of retiring from the sea. He had chartered *Zaidie* and was sailing with his wife and a young hand from the yard, who spent most of his time sick in the fo'c'sle. Taylor greeted us uproariously on our arrival, and we had lots to talk about as it was some thirty years since I had last seen him (at Colintraive on my first cruise in a dreadful old boat which four of us had chartered for five pounds a month). As he was keen to go north, but had no charts north of Mull, I sealed our friendship by giving him my Skye charts, which he duly returned when he came later to Rhu.

Another hard-sailed boat was the 1927 " 19/24 " *Trebor*. The day we had lain storm-stayed at Canna in 1932 she had made a remarkably fast, and far too adventurous passage from Kyle Akin, sixty-one miles in eight and a half hours. Reid was having a well-earned rest when we found him at Tobormory on our arrival next day. He confessed to having been a bit anxious off Ardnamurchan with the heavy seas, a strong north-westerly, a shaky transom, and a seasick wife the only other person on board.

We had been unfortunate in missing *Fiara* in 1931, but luckily found her here in 1933.

There were larger cruisers also : *Morna* (R.C.C.), *Ron II*, *Fedoa*, and one very large ship, the three-masted schooner *Aldebaran*, ex *Meteor III*, flying the American ensign. Still larger was the French research ship, *Pourquoi Pas* (lost in the Arctic some years later), and sundry steamers, S.S. *Killarney*, *Glen Shiel*, and two or three " Vital Sparks." Several of H.M. ships were there also, but of their activities I should not write. There were, of course, a few " gin palaces," smart, oh, very smart motor cruisers ; one of them actually complete with a uniformed house-maid on board.

The oldest ship in the bay was the Spanish galleon, *Florida*, but out of sight, out of mind, and not even the youngest member of the crew wanted to try his luck with a grapnel.

An interesting thing about the arrival of boats was that they just suddenly appeared, unless one caught a glimpse of them through the Doirlinn Narrows if coming up the Sound, or when walking along the cliff path to the Runa Gal Lighthouse had seen them coming in from outside.

Those I have mentioned were not, of course, all in at the same time, but no matter how many there were there was lots of room. The bay is large and well-sheltered by Calve I. although in northerly winds one feels the swell even when anchored well in off the old pier. We were inclined to make this the excuse, if we had no other, for crossing over to Loch Drumbuy, and we soon became very familiar with the scattered group of rocks, the New, the Red and the Stirks, which lie between Tobormory and Loch Sunart.

Before leaving Tobormory I must pay a compliment to the Town Clock ! As we were finishing a game of family bridge one night our chronometer, the Town Clock and Big Ben on the wireless all struck the hour of midnight absolutely simultaneously ; so we just had to turn in.

Loch Drumbuy

The entrance to this land-locked bay is a straight narrow channel, steep-to on both sides, with no obstructions except a six-feet shoal on the south side just after opening out the loch itself. So one should keep to the north side until past the second point on port.

The most convenient anchorage is in the bay on the south, as there is a burn here and a fine stretch of short grass, both of which my wife found very useful when doing " a big washing." As the shore shoals one has to be well out to get six or seven fathoms. No matter how hard it is blowing outside there is complete and absolute peace in here as the bay is surrounded by high, wooded hills.

Our first entrance in 1930 was quite a thrill, as none of us knew what to expect, but soon after anchoring our pleasure was marred by an accident. The two youngest had bought mascots in Tobormory and were seeing how high up the mast they could climb with them, when Neill slipping, fell a good twelve feet through the open forehatch. I found him on the fo'c'sle floor completely knocked out with a nasty scalp wound which was bleeding freely. As I carried on board a good outfit of dressings, instruments, etc. ("just in case,") I wasted no time in attending to his injury with the assistance of Bob, the medical student. But the hot stuffy atmosphere of the cabin, or perhaps the sight of his young brother's blood, was too much for Bob, who gradually subsided on to the floor. As my hands were full, Charlie, the engineer, helped him out into the cockpit and with apparent stoical indifference took his place.

I did not sleep well that night as I found Neill's bunk too small—he was in his mother's bed and she had mine—and I was naturally worried about the lad.

Taylor, who had told us of this place when we met him at Puillodobhrain, came in in *Frolic* later in the evening and was sorry to hear of our misadventure.

Next day we took things quietly, all except my wife and the patient sailing in *Bud* to the other end of the loch. Charlie, Bob and I splashed in the evening and " got horribly wet and caught only one dog-fish and many crabs." We managed with difficulty to keep Neill in bed for one day, but after that he was running about with the others ashore, his head well bandaged but apparently none the worse for his fall.

When after two days here we were reluctantly preparing to leave, " Billy," who had been taken ashore, could not be found. We searched all round the bay without success, and were returning to the boat undecided as to what we should do when we heard him barking. But as soon as we got near him he stopped barking and we were no further on. After this manœuvre had been repeated several times my wife by chance saw his eyes shining in a hole under a decayed tree stump. He had been trapped when rabbiting by a large stone which he had dislodged.

We were back here again the following year, 1931, and visited the farm at Dorlinn, walking along the rough road which comes across from Drimnin on the Sound of Mull. From the farm there is a path, and a poor path at that, to the entrance to Loch Teachdais inside Charna where there is an iron signpost marked " Drimnin." Who put it there, and when and why, and why is it pointing northwards across Loch Sunart?

We caught five sea trout and a dozen mackerel the evening we arrived, so we are not cured yet, but we are careful to restrict our illegal activities to places where nobody objects.

(We left next morning for the North, but got no further than Canna.)

When running up the Sound of Mull from Loch Aline in 1932 we heard en passant from *Lady Bridgella* (the late Arthur Hedderwick) that the Robertsons in *Gigha* were lying in Drumbuy. (We had lost her after leaving Craobh, Loch Shuna some ten days before.) So we slipped in ever so quietly, and not until we had anchored beside them did any of them appear. We then heard that at their first attempt to get through Cuan Sound, having missed the entrance, they had gone aground in Balvicar Bay, and when getting through at their second shot had hit the Cleit Rock before being vomited out into a strong north-westerly, which worried them considerably. We went across to Tobormory to get stores and pick up Charlie, but came back to Drumbuy next day to celebrate our reunion by a most successful dinner party on our ship.

Loch Sunart, Charna

When *Gigha* left for the south we motored round to Loch Sunart in driving mist and anchored between Oronsay and Eil. nan Eildean, in the channel west of Charna, opposite the deserted Dorlinn cottage. In the afternoon we rowed to outer Loch Teachdais and walked to Rahoy, the home of Mary's friend N.N., and when coming back inspected the remains of a vitrified fort. As there was a strong wind with poor visibility, we stayed put next day, but in the evening the sky cleared and there was a wonderfully beautiful sunset. As the evening forecast was good, we hoped to get off next day for the North.

(We left early next morning and after a long day arrived at Loch na Beist.)

Loch Sunart, Salen

In 1933 we were held up at Tobormory for a couple of days waiting for favourable weather. It was difficult to withstand " a combined assault by the whole crew who demanded to sail round Ardnamurchan in spite of a strong southerly, a falling glass and very unsettled weather." So I fell back on the unfailing solution and crossed over to Drumbuy, where my caution was justified when *Grace*, who had left for the north heavily reefed, came in having " had more than enough." We must have had a long lie that night as Bob got eleven hours uninterrupted sleep in the deckhouse. As it was still blowing hard we went round to Salen under mizzen and jib, anchoring just north-east of the stone pier in five fathoms. Some walked to Acharacle, Loch Shiel ; the rest of us just " cleaned up." We tried unsuccessfully to phone Charlie ; we then wired him but got no reply.

The glass was still falling next day, but we motored in mist through the Laudale Narrows, and hoisting all sail beat to Strontian at the head of the loch. Running back we had a look at an anchorage between Eil. Garbh and Rudha an Daimh, the " dries ten-feet " rock just showing at one and a half hours ebb, and then explored the " gut " on the north of Oronsay before making Tobormory close-hauled with the last of the breeze. As we were now waiting for Charlie we spent the next day, Mary's eighteenth birthday, sailing across to Mingary, where we spent some hours at the old Castle. It is an imposing ruin, with a sea-gate leading down to the rocks.

We rolled a lot that night, but endured it as Charlie was due to arrive by the *M.V. Loch Fyne* in the morning.

Loch Sunart, " The Gut," Oronsay

On our return from the north nine days later, after laying in stores at Tobormory, we went to the Gut, anchoring in two fathoms opposite the gap between the small islet on port and Oronsay. The bay seemed full of duck and seals, whom we tried unsuccessfully to stalk with a camera. Although it blew during the night we had swinging room—just. (See p. 103). We went back next day to Tobormory to meet *Fiara* and with her, after a night at Drumbuy, sailed to Eil. Garbh.

Loch Sunart, Eil. Garbh

We found a good spot in four fathoms behind the island. The young people climbed Ben Resipol, but Kathleen and Mary did not reach the top. As it was blowing " fresh " straight into the bay next morning, we shifted round under mizzen and jib to Salen. We anchored further in this time, off the tin boat house, and as the wind took off in the evening, were very comfortable.

46

V

Round Ardnamurchan

THE difficulties and dangers of the passage round Ardnamurchan have perhaps been exaggerated, but they undoubtedly exist. As the Point is quite exposed to the west, there is always a heavy sea in " fresh " westerly winds, and although there are no inshore dangers it is advisable to give it a good berth. Further north after passing Muck the seas are apt to be short and broken over Maxwell Bank where there are only eight to ten fathoms.

Although the flood at Ardnamurchan is only one and a half knots Springs, it increases in the Sound of Sleat and should, if possible, be taken advantage of.

But for *Rowan II*, who is admittedly slow to windward, the chief problems are the direction and strength of the wind. With a long passage—thirty-three miles to Mallaig, or forty-one to Isle Ornsay—one is inclined to start early when, in summer at least, it is difficult to forecast the day's weather. Lying in the quiet shelter of Tobormory or Drumbuy one cannot guess what it will be like at Ardnamurchan some ten miles to the west about two hours later. The 10.30 a.m. weather forecast, if one waits for it, should help, but we found that while this was generally accurate over wide areas, it seldom gave any warning of the unexpected and sudden local changes so often experienced in these quarters.

Going North

What we wanted was a wind from south to something west of north, and moderate in strength. If after passing the Point the wind was east of north, it meant windward work usually against a rising sea and that was not to our liking. Eigg was, it is true, only eleven miles away, but it offered little shelter in northerly winds ; Mallaig, thirteen miles further on, was no better. (If one had punched as far as this the wise course was to persevere another eight miles to a comfortable anchorage in Inverie Bay, Loch Nevis ; a disturbed night, in 1933, at Mallaig taught us this.)

If conditions at Ardnamurchan were unfavourable there were two alternatives. One could turn south through the Passage of Tiree and make for Gometra or Ulva, but during the flood, and we had probably counted on that, there is a bad rip off Caliach Point, especially with a northerly. Or one could call it a day and run back to Tobormory or Drumbuy, but this certainly would not meet with the approval of a crew like mine.

Coming South

This was a much simpler business and gave us no trouble. When waiting till southerly winds had taken off (if one had time to wait) one could lie in Isle Ornsay or Canna, or even in Mallaig, or safely, but perhaps not comfortably, in Eigg, and then with a very good idea of the prospects of the day run the thirty or fewer miles to Ardnamurchan. If the northerly, for which we had waited, veered to north-east and increased in strength, the stretch from the Plough Rock might be distinctly " stoory " as the squalls from Ben Hiant can be very strong, but by that time we would be in quieter water.

Rowan II's Three Passages, North and South

Going North

In 1931 we left Drumbuy at 7 a.m. on a lovely morning, the sun shining over Ben Resipol and the loch like a mirror. We got a light breeze at Ardnamurchan, but as it was north-easterly and would mean a long beat up the Sound of Sleat, we decided on Canna as our destination. The wind, however, backed through north to north-west, and we had a beat after all and it was 5 p.m. before we made Canna, the wind then being distinctly " fresh."

In 1932 having lain at Charna for two nights because of strong westerly winds with poor visibility, I got up at 4.45 a.m., and while Charlie was taking " Jack " ashore, and Bob was having his usual dip, I lifted not only the anchor but also an enormous mass of seaweed. We got away at 5.15 a.m. under engine as there was not a breath of wind. I served early tea to the crew ; my wife rose off Kilchoan, followed soon after by John and Neill ; Mary did not put in an appearance till we were at the Point of Sleat at noon. From Ardnamurchan to Eigg we had dense mist and made use of our elementary navigational studies. From Eigg we were able to do without the engine and beat to Isle Ornsay with a fine north-easterly which was increasing all the time. As we were too early for the tide at Kyle Rhea we reduced our speed by dropping the mainsail, and had tea in peace, and then getting through against the last of the ebb anchored at the head of Loch na Beist at 8 p.m. nearly fifteen hours out from Charna.

In 1933 Charlie joined us at Tobormory, and as soon as he had stepped off the *Loch Fyne* we had him on board, and within a few minutes we were off under engine. At Ardnamurchan Point we shut off the engine, and carrying a light north-wester made Eigg in one board. The wind then failed and we spent the next hour drifting, while the young people played games on the deck, my wife sketched and the rest of us just " lazed about." When we were peacefully having tea I at the tiller saw that the weather was changing, and almost before the cups and plates were stowed we were punching into a northerly, which soon increased to " fresh," if not " strong," and kicked up a really big sea. With the wind veering to north-east we were getting down to leeward off Arisaig, a part of the coast we did not fancy, so we put on the engine (we had already pulled down a reef) and punched our way to Mallaig arriving there in heavy rain thoroughly soaked by both fresh and salt water.

Coming South

In 1931 we were lying at Totaig, Loch Duich with *Morna*, both of us south-bound. I got up at 6 a.m. hoping to steal a march on Workman, but found the loch enveloped in dense mist. We tried to slip out without being heard, but the engine gave us away and we were greeted by jeers from the Irishmen. On clearing Eil. Aoinidh we managed to pick up the north shore at Ais-sgeir, the rock used as a guide to the channel, but I was properly told off for steering W.N.W. instead of N.W. by W., the course laid off by Charlie. We then groped our way across Nostie Bay, but as the mist was absolutely thick all round we anchored off a white cottage with a red roof, which we saw just in time before we ran ashore. We had breakfast and hoped that *Morna* had not heard us anchoring.

At noon the mist lifted and getting through Kyle Rhea with the last of the ebb, we found a fine north-westerly off Isle

Ornsay and soon had Eigg abeam. We thought we were going to have an easy passage round Ardnamurchan, but before we reached Muck we were getting more wind and sea than we wanted, so pulling down a reef, we turned back to *Eigg*. I had heard a lot about the anchorage here from a man at Dornie, who claimed to have " local knowledge," but having passed between the two perches, the tops of which were just showing, we very nearly came to grief. I had been advised to anchor off the north jetty, and it was only due to Bob's prompt warning that we did not pile up on the rocks. We then found our way out and anchored between the south jetty and Eil. Castle. Within a few hours the bay we had been in had dried out. We were lucky as it was high water Springs, and had we gone ashore, well, who knows when we would have got off. (As the result of a note I sent to the Clyde Cruising Club this north jetty has been expunged from the sketch plan in the 1937 edition of the Journal.)

After our sheltered anchorages up north we felt very exposed here and early next morning, after Charlie had attended to the engine which was " full of water," and Bob had been over the side, we left under power. It was dead calm and " the scene when the sun rose was perfect ; the masses of mist on the mountains of Rum and Skye ; the dark shadows on the hills of the bay and the sunlit summit of the Scuir." With a light south-westerly we had a pleasant sail to Tobormory, where we got letters and stores before crossing to Drumbuy. We then celebrated our safe return from our first cruise " up North " by a huge dinner, an early bedding and a long lie.

In 1932 after two days at Canna, when a gale warning was justified by strong winds, I looked out early and " finding all things good " decided to move. We carried a fine northerly to Ardnamurchan, but after that had a slow run in a failing wind to Tobormory.

In 1933 we left Loch na Beist on a lovely morning, beat through Kyle Rhea with the engine " ticking over," looked into Loch Hourn, Loch Nevis and Mallaig, and losing the light south-westerly at Eigg had to rely entirely on the Handy-billy. We then played the good Samaritan by towing *Trebor* (who said he had been drifting about for days between Muck and Ardnamurchan) for four hours to Tobormory.

VI

Ardnamurchan to Gairloch

Eigg

I HAVE already indicated that this anchorage, between the south jetty and Eil. Castle may be useful, but it may also be most uncomfortable. The island certainly gives shelter from winds from south to east, and Eigg itself from winds from north to west, but in both cases one is apt to be held by the wind across the tide which runs through at three to four knots Springs. Again, winds from north-east and south-west blow straight through the funnel, and although Garbh Sgeir helps to break anything from the north-east there is nothing to keep out a heavy sea from the south-west. That sounds very complicated but is well worth remembering before choosing this as one's anchorage.

One may enter from the south, keeping clear of the reef off the Eigg shore, or from the north between the two perches. These may be difficult to pick up at high water Springs, especially the one on port which will be almost awash. The holding is good—one must give the place one good mark. The people ashore also are very friendly ; there is no feeling that the island is " private " like Rum. There is water at the jetty, but it is a long two miles to the small store.

As we did not linger there on our way home in 1931 we did not have time to see the cave where the hunchbacked MacLeod murdered about four hundred of the inhabitants in 1577, nor did we walk to the " singing sands " in the Bay of Laig. But we could not help being impressed by the great Scuir which seems to stand over the bay like an enormous tower, or to be resting on the island like a gigantic prehistoric monster.

Mallaig

As there are usually many tiers of trawlers, drifters, etc. lying alongside the pier, a mere yacht has to keep well out in the bay where with anything from the north there is no shelter and a considerable sea comes rolling in. When we arrived in 1933, after a very wet windward punch, we were hailed by two of my nieces, and as they did not leave the ship till midnight we decided to stay where we were even though it promised to be uncomfortable. But long before morning we were sorry we had not gone on to Loch Nevis as we pitched all night and the grinding of the angel on the chain kept my wife awake. So we said " never again," but as usual did not keep to our resolve and experienced a similar discomfort on a future occasion.

Mallaig has been called " The Slum of the Highlands " and " the place of herring-guts and seagulls," and while it does not deserve these insults it is certainly not without smell and smoke. But what else could one expect from a fishing port and a railway terminus ? If one is short of stores or has to telephone or wishes to pick up one of the crew, or perhaps to get rid of one, it is a useful port of call, but having finished one's business there it would be wise to lift anchor and push on to Inverie Bay, Loch Nevis for peace and comfort.

Isle Ornsay

About eight miles up the Sound of Sleat from Mallaig is an excellent harbour behind Isle Ornsay. In 1931, having run from Scathvaig to the Point of Sleat we had beaten against a good north-easterly up the Sound and anchored just inside the line from the north point of the island to the church. The head of the bay shoals far out and even though we had only three fathoms we seemed a long way from the shore. The evening forecast spoke of fresh to strong north winds, and it blew hard during the night, but with fifteen fathoms out and an angel we were quite comfortable. The squalls from the Skye hills are very strong and require to be watched in northerly winds.

When ashore in the evening we had found that several families had scarlet fever, so we left early next morning to get through Kyle Rhea with the first of the flood. At Kyle of Loch Alsh, where we got stores, we had a look outside, but as the northerly was distinctly fresh and visibility very poor we ran back to Totaig, Loch Duich, negotiating the passage north of Glas Eilean without difficulty.

Totaig, Loch Duich

This is a small bay at the entrance to one of the most beautiful of Scotland's lochs, with the " Five Sisters of Kintail," four of them well over 3,000 feet, forming a grand background. The best spot is half-way between the island and the fence on the west side (if you can see it !) and as there is little swinging-room it is advisable to slip an angel down the chain.

In addition to scenic beauty there is much of historic interest here centred chiefly round Eilean Donnan Castle, a fine building on the east side of the narrows. The original castle was built more than 700 years ago on the side of a vitrified fort. In 1719, when some Spanish troops with a body of Seaforths were defeated by the Royalist forces at the Battle of Glen Shiel, it was bombarded by H.M. *Worcester* and several cannon balls may still be seen embedded in the walls. After that it remained in ruins until recently restored by (the late) Col. MacRae Gilstrap, one of whose ancestors was at one time its Constable. The restoration has been remarkably well done, but my wife wonders how the domestic arrangements in what is really a medieval castle can be satisfactorily solved to-day.

On the high ground above Flounder Bay (where we failed to catch flounders or anything else) is an even older building, a Celtic broch. This not nearly so well preserved as those at Glenelg. only the lower part of the wall remaining. But it still shows the carefully laid, undressed stones forming a double wall about twelve feet thick in which there are several galleries. The doorway has checks for a door and bar-holes behind them ; there is also a guard chamber off the passage. There is a fine view through the doorway, which faces north-east, past Dornie up Loch Long, which like its namesake on the Clyde is long and narrow.

We stayed here in 1931 for four days, as although the weather was fine and the glass steady the fresh northerly continued to blow. We did indeed make one half-hearted attempt to leave one day as the wind seemed to be veering, but the " strong north-west with quite a big sea " that we found at the lighthouse at Kyle gave us a good excuse for returning.

The days passed far too quickly as will be seen from some of the log entries : " a picnic tea ashore ; then a lovely walk to Letterfearn two miles up the loch, getting milk and seeing kennels and sheep-shearing ; back for a huge dinner including a ' glassed chicken,' our first preserved meat this cruise ; the Five Sisters at the head of the loch most perfect in the evening sunlight, each with a wisp of soft white cloud half-way down like a scarf ; quite decided to stay here for days and days ; with Charlie and Bob had a very sporting sail in the dinghy to Dornie where we saw the lady with whom they had stayed last October when on a motor tour ; a day of glorious sunshine ; we all went across to Dornie and saw over the Castle with the aid of a big Highlander, whose stockings interested us immensely ; hunted up the butcher, whose ' shop ' was a tiny wooden hut in the village, but who lived some miles up Loch Long ; as he was still in bed when we found him, it was some time before we got any meat ; on our return Mother did a big washing ashore, the clothes being hung over the bushes to dry ; a walk to Ratagan after a nap ; back for a big dinner at 8 p.m. ; Neill swam round the yacht in the morning and caught a 3-lb. cod in the evening ; Bob dived under the yacht, thereby displaying great moral courage ; in the afternoon walked almost to Ardintoul Bay and were chagrined to see a light southerly which would have served us well for Portree."

And when we at last decided to leave " Billy " had other plans, and it was only after a long search that we found him.

Loch na Beist

I must not altogether neglect this anchorage which is popular with those who are in such a hurry to get north that they do not turn aside into such lovely spots as Totaig. We were in here twice ; in 1932 after a long day from Loch Sunart, and in 1933 on our way south from Portree.

The anchorage is at the head of the bay off a burn, and it is difficult to get less than seven fathoms. It is quite isolated and the walk over the hill to Kyle Akin is both arduous and wet. No ! Totaig is far better, and after all it is not much off one's course north or south.

IN FULL BLOSSOM—1929-1934

Portree

During these three years we were in Portree only twice. The first time was in 1931 after a pleasant sail from Totaig, but we stayed only long enough to get some stores before going on to Acarsaid Mor, South Rona, which a friendly fisherman strongly recommended.

The second time, in 1933, having had a hard beat from Loch Torridon down the Inner Sound, through Caol Rona and down Raasay Sound, we were glad to get into a quiet anchorage where we could replenish our rapidly diminishing stores. As the bay reminded us of Tobormory and the swell which may disturb one there, we lashed the dinghy alongside and carefully adjusted the cat-harpings before turning in. It was here that we first met Mrs. McGrigor Phillips who was flying the R.C.C. burgee on her fine yacht *Sea Swallow* (ex *Tern IV*.)

Portree is tucked round a corner, and to get to the anchorage, which remains hidden until one is well in, one may have to beat against strong baffling squalls from the high cliffs which guard the entrance.

It has been called the Capital of Skye, and is a most convenient centre from which, if storm-stayed, to visit Sligachan, Dunvegan, Duntulm and the Quiraing, passing on the way that strange isolated rock, the " Old Man of Storr," which stands out on the side of the hill. The name Portree is usually thought to mean Port Righ or the Port of the King, so-called to commemorate a visit in 1540 by James V. But others hold that it is Port Righeadh, the harbour of the slope. The lay-out of the town, the row of houses beside the pier and the steep road leading up to the town itself high up on the ridge overlooking the bay, seems to support this. Below there were fishermen sitting on the wharf looking at the harbour, and above the townspeople, farmers, and of course, tourists.

Acarsaid Mor, S. Rona

As the fisherman at Portree was himself going to Acarsaid Mor, he offered to show us the way in, but with full sail and a fair wind we soon left him far behind, and getting safely into the " Big Harbour " in a blatter of wind and rain had found a perfect anchorage behind the island before he arrived.

Cowper's warning that " this is a port only to be attempted by those ardent mariners who have failed to get wrecked when attempting others equally difficult," is absurd, but there is undoubtedly need for care. The entrance is a little difficult to pick up as Rough I., which should be passed on port, is so like the rough hummocks of Rona itself. But there is a definite landmark, the house at the head of the bay, and as soon as this is seen the channel is easily identified. (See later on p. 119 how in 1937 a little carelessness led us astray.)

The channel itself is a bit tricky ; the perches which should mark the two rocks are unreliable, they may or may not be there. Chart 2570 (northern part of Sound of Raasay and Inner Sound) is the best guide in spite of its insistence on the existence of the " Widow's Cot " which disappeared long ago. Even an experienced sailor like G. I. Taylor came to grief in *Frolic* here in 1924. Making sure that he would not touch the first rock on port (it covers at three and a half hours' flood) he got on to the rocky shore on starboard. As it was high water and the tides were taking off, it was only after two very anxious days and with the help of the Macraes that he got off without damage. But then he was, after his fashion, entering for the first time at midnight.

" Rona " is Norse for rough, and the character of the island bears this out. It is a collection of desolate rough rocky hummocks, some bare, some sparsely covered with heather. According to Martin " this little isle is the most unequal rocky piece of ground to be seen anywhere." And in 1549 Munro, " The High Dean of the Isles," wrote that it was " full of wood and hedder, with ane havin for heiland gallys in the middis of it, and the same havein is guyed for fostering of theives, ruggairs, and reivairs, till a nail, upon the peilling and spulzeing of poure pepill. This ile pertains to M'Gilly-challan of Raarsay by force, and to the bishope of the iles be heritage."

The island was almost deserted in 1919 when the " Raasay Raiders " left. Only one family remained, the Macraes who, as is the custom in the Highlands, consider themselves " strangers," as although more than thirty years in Rona they had come originally from Loch Duich.

LOOKING NORTH FROM EASDALE

ST. MUNGO ISLAND, LOCH LEVEN

DUART CASTLE, SOUND OF MULL

ISLE ORNSAY, SOUND OF SLEAT

DUNVEGAN CASTLE

"THE TINKER'S HOLE," ERRAID, F S OF MUI

Rowan III RACING AT GOUROCK

While the rest of the company were paying the Macraes a visit I, with "Billy," was isolated on a hillock ringed round by a herd of what I thought were wild bulls. I did not realize that it was the dog they were annoyed at, not me. After my rescue we all walked to Acarsaid Tioram and saw the deserted "township" with the primitive little church and school-house just as they had been left twelve years before. There were still school-books on the benches and writing on the blackboard. In the evening we had a magnificent view from the top of a hill, the mountains of Skye to the south, to the west the north of Skye, the Shiants and Lewis, and to the east the shore and mountains of Ross and Cromarty.

Loch Torridon

After our first visit to Acarsaid Mor, in 1931, we had turned south, but in 1933 we went on from there to Loch Torridon, having a fast run in misty weather with a moderate south-westerly. We anchored in Loch Creagach, off the clachan of *Kenmore*. "A lovely evening; all except the Skipper, who stayed to tidy up, write letters and get some peace, walked to Arrina-crinnach for stores, but got nothing; we have only half a loaf left now; the Mate spent the evening buying home-spun wool for stockings and had difficulty in arranging payment as there seemed to be no change in the small clachan."

Next day we sailed to the head of Upper Loch Torridon and then beat into the narrow gut between Shieldaig I. and the village. Leaving Charlie and Bob on board the rest of us went ashore for much needed stores and were caught by a very violent thunderstorm and got thoroughly soaked rowing back. I was relieved to see that the two on board had veered out a lot more chain as the squalls were very fierce and the anchor was in sand. While Loch Creagach is sheltered from all except easterly winds, Shieldaig is exposed to the north even if one goes almost as far in as Sgeir Shalach close to the island.

Badachro, Gairloch

It was in the previous year, 1932, that we came here after a fast passage in an easterly up the Inner Sound. (I seem to have missed out Plockton, Loch Carron, where we spent a night, but as my wife and I were there some years later, I will pass over it just now.) (See page 159) Off Ru Ruag we saw in the distance what looked like a fleet of lugsails, but on going out to investigate found that they were basking sharks. There were so many pupils in the " school," and they were frolicking about in such an unusual and alarming fashion, that after taking some photos we were glad to resume our course.

Dropping the mainsail we came in to Badachro under mizzen and jib holding well over to the Horrisdale I. side of the narrow passage. We anchored in two fathoms between Dry I. and the " dries 12-feet " rock. Although this rock is marked on Chart 3441 (Loch Gairloch) it has been omitted in the sketch plan in the C.C.C. Journal.

VII

Round Skye

HAVING come from Gareloch to Gairloch, our furthest north, we decided to celebrate Mary's seventeenth birthday by sailing round Skye.

Before a light easterly we sailed out of the loch, but it soon failed and we lay for an hour slamming about in the swell. Then quite suddenly, as is the custom in these parts, a decidedly "fresh" northerly sprang up and we soon had a reef rolled down. As I had sprained my right wrist rather badly the day before and felt less inclined for heavy manual work, and perhaps even more easily irritated than usual, I suggested that we should give up our project and run down to Portree. But thanks chiefly to Charlie's enthusiasm we carried on.

I realized that with the fresh northerly against the two and a half knot flood there would be a nasty rip as soon as we got to Trodday, and quite wrongly thought that it would be less outside than between the island and Trotternish Point. As soon as we had passed Trodday, on port, we saw our mistake as we got into a really bad rip with steep seas between it and Fladdachuain. ('Fladda of the Ocean').

There was so much broken water that it was only after a very careful scrutiny of the chart that we were satisfied that we were on our proper course and were not heading for rocks. Even the usually phlegmatic Bob thought it was "very impressive." For a quarter of an hour *Berry* was in great danger, but, thanks to a long painter from a shackle at the water-line, came through safely although by no means dry.

To reduce our speed we rolled down another reef, and after passing Yesker, as the wind was now north-east and with the big sea there was a danger of gybing, we shifted from mainsail to trysail. Keeping well off Vaternish Point, as the flood was still strong, we ran into quieter water, and after a meal hoisted full sail again at Isay I. When finally drifting up Loch Dunvegan with the last of the breeze, Bob was playing the pipes on the foredeck and was lustily cheered by the crews of four fishing boats on their way out.

We anchored in most beautiful surroundings below the Castle exactly twelve hours out from Badachro; a fine sail under constantly changing conditions.

Dunvegan

We slept soundly after our long day, but my wife had the rest of the crew ashore soon after breakfast inspecting the Castle which, standing high on a rocky promontory overlooking the loch, is most imposing. Although this ancestral home of the MacLeods dates back to the thirteenth century, or even earlier, very little of the original building remains. At first access was only by a narrow staircase leading up from the Water Gate, but there is now an entrance by a bridge across the surrounding ravine. They saw the dungeon, really just a pit, with a grill so arranged that its unfortunate starving inmates could smell the cooked food which was being taken to the dining hall. A very interesting relic was the " Fairy Flag," which was supposed to have been brought home from the Holy Land by a crusading MacLeod, and if unfurled, would bring help in time of need—but three times only. It is now a flimsy rag and has evidently lost its magic power, as it is preserved in a glass case.

Dunvegan is also famed for its hereditary pipers, the Mac-Crimmons, who for centuries had a college of piping at Boreraig on the west side of the loch.

While the rest of the ship's company were delving into the past I was attending to our present needs by visiting the store. I was astonished on my way back to be accosted by a Customs Officer, who asked if I was the " master and owner of the yacht in the bay," and if I had any dutiable goods on board. He very courteously refused my invitation to come on board and sample one of them ! Is the recent partition of Ireland to blame for this unexpected official activity ?

I was interested later to read in Martin's book that " Skye, in the ancient language Skianach, i.e. winged, is so called because the two opposite northern promontories (Vaterness lying north-west, and Trotterness north-east) resemble two wings."

He also gives a very interesting note on the influence of the weather in the island on the habits of the natives and those

DUNVEGAN CASTLE. See photograph, page 59.

who may visit it. " The air here is commonly moist and cold. This disposes the inhabitants to take a larger dose of brandy or other strong liquors than in the south of Scotland, by which they fancy that they qualify the moisture of the air. This is the opinion of all strangers, as well as of the natives, since the one as well as the other drinks at least treble the quantity of brandy in Skye and the adjacent isles that they do in the more southern climate." Not merely an excuse but an explanation !

In the afternoon we went by car to Skiabost to visit our late cook in her mother's small thatched cottage. We left for Canna next morning.

Canna

From Dunvegan to Canna we had the usual varied conditions —a light north-easterly at the start, then a spell of no wind under The Sgor, heavy squalls off the cliffs at Gob na Hoe, and then a steadily increasing northerly to Canna. We foolishly thought we could manœuvre into our anchorage under mizzen and jib and got into rather a muddle out of which the immediate response of the Handybilly took us.

Soon after we had anchored it was blowing " strong," and next morning my wife said it had been " a wild night," but thanks to the fresh air and an angel the rest of us had had " an absolutely peaceful night." As it was now blowing hard and raining heavily we spent most of the day on board, but after dinner, which included three lobsters, visited the Thoms. On the following morning we left early and had a pleasant run with a moderate northerly to Tobormory, where we found about a dozen other yachts including the redoubtable *Trebor*.

We had been in Canna once before, on our way north in 1931, and had been greatly interested in this our first port north of Ardnamurchan, as these extracts from the log indicate : " after a cup of tea and many biscuits we went ashore ; saw the six by six-feet store, but got nothing in it ; a very old cross on what is said to be the site of a chapel connected in some way with St. Columba ; a big ' agglomerate stack ' with some ruins on the top and a romantic story attached ; Compass Hill with its evil magnetic influence ; came on board absolutely famished ; had an enormous five-course dinner, which the ' stewardess ' produced in half an hour ; ate and drank till 10 p.m. ; played bridge till midnight when rolling on to our couches we were all immediately fast asleep."

Next morning we paid our respects to the Thom family and I see from the log that "the Skipper transformed his disreputable appearance in three minutes by means of two studs, a collar, an R.C.C. tie and a sports jacket." Mr. Thom showed my wife his private Memorial Church with its stone roof, and myself the way to get into the anchorage at Scathvaig.

Loch Scathvaig

As it was on our way north, in 1931, that we came here from Canna, reference to it should find no place in the account of our journey round Skye, but I must not miss it out (as I did Plockton), and I cannot think where else to put it in.

There is no large scale chart of Loch Scathvaig, the only one in which it appears, almost as if with a grudge at the margin, is 2507 (Ardnamurchan Point to Loch Brittle, Skye) and the Pilot too is not helpful.

But using the excellent sketch plan in the C.C.C. Journal, we had no difficulty in getting in, at dead low water, to the land-locked bay behind Eil. Glas. The only notes I made about the entrance were : Eil. Reamhar is a considerable island covered with grass not a rock ; Sgeir Doghigh is merely a bare rock, not an island ; the rock, which dries five feet west of Eil. Glas, is nearer the island than the half-cable mentioned in the Pilot, and is best passed to starboard ; do not turn to starboard till well through the channel to clear the rock off the north corner of the island ; we found the burn tumbling down the hillside from Sgurr Alasdair at the north-west corner of the Bay useful in fixing our position.

The entries in the log are scanty ; I had no inclination to write much ; " we bathed from the yacht ; we walked to Loch Coruisk and to the ' Bad Step ' on the path to Camasunary ; a man who was "splashing" when we came in warned us that the mouth of the river was closely watched at night, so although the salmon and sea trout were jumping there the splash net remained below ; Bob was piping on the Island in the evening greatly to the perturbation of a boat full of watchers who seemed to suspect that he was some sort of sentinel."

I will make no attempt to describe the grandeur, the magnificent beauty of this place. It was peaceful when we were there and yet at night the stillness and solitude was quite eerie. Surrounded, overshadowed, in fact enveloped by the wild mountains, it is easy to imagine how awesome it may be.

VIII

Mull to Rhu, Round " The Mull "

THE day after our return from Skye to Tobormory the crew, who seemed to be infected by a circum-navigational bacillus, insisted on sailing round Mull in spite of a morning forecast of a depression south-east of the Hebrides with fresh north or west winds.

We had a quiet beat out of the Sound of Mull, meeting *Ron II* running up from the south, but off Loch Cuan there were heavy rain squalls with black clouds to windward. As usual I suggested turning back, but as usual Charlie prevailed on me to go on. I agreed so long as we were round Caliach Point before the flood started. We rolled down a reef and, although we gave the point a good offing, found a very confused broken sea due to the last of the two-knot ebb running against the rising wind which had backed to west.

Bailachloidh Harbour, Gometra

After passing the point we had a fast reach between Carraig Dubh and the Treshnish Isles, and then a run past Moisgeir, keeping well off its south end. Approaching the entrance to Bailachloidh Harbour, although the flood was only one hour old (three days after Springs), we saw no sign of the " dries four-feet " Bogha Ludden, but picking up the " dries nine-feet " Sgeir na Skeineadh took the passage between it and Rudha Bhrigheadh and found our way in easily.

Dropping anchor in six fathoms opposite the jetty on the west side of the bay, we went ashore for a walk. A fisherman told me that further in off a cliff on the Ulva side there was better holding in mud, so after getting " chickens, eggs and lobsters," we shifted across.

Bunessan, Loch Lathaich

Next morning we left for Staffa with a fair wind, but as we were not able to land there owing to the swell, bore away for Loch Lathaich. We got a very heavy rain squall outside the loch, but, being now very expert at the job, we rolled down a reef as we saw it coming and rehoisted as soon as it had passed. Keeping Grey I. to starboard we ran in behind White I. and anchored in three fathoms off the stone pier. " One party ashore for stores ; later another party ashore for what the first party had forgotten."

My wife said that during the night there was " a continuous roar of wind as if high up," but although there certainly were many rain squalls we were well sheltered as the wind was northerly. But I think that this bay being wide open to the north might be very uncomfortable, even when behind the island, if there was much sea outside. (see p. 141).

We left Bunessan in a " fresh " northerly with a reef down and were soon in the Sound of Iona, but finding the flood strong off the " landing place " we anchored in the " Bull Hole " between Eil. nam ban and the Ross of Mull, opposite the dip in the island. I laid a kedge as although we intended moving on after visiting Iona the ebb was due to start in three hours.

We walked to Fionnphort ; crossed in the ferry ; were delighted to meet Sister M. just home on holiday from Glasgow ; had lunch ; " saw everything of interest," which I will not attempt to describe ; and were then ferried back direct to the yacht by Capt. MacDonald who agreed with me that " The Tinker's Hole " would be more comfortable than where we were. The " Bull Hole " may be very safe, but the run of the tide is bound to be a nuisance and one could not lie comfortably to a single anchor.

" The Tinker's Hole," Erraid, Ross of Mull

Running down the Sound, under mizzen and jib, we had some difficulty in identifying the various boghas and sgeirs which are so much alike. Charlie and I had a furious argument about Eil. nam Muc due to the position of the name on the chart in relation to the actual island. I was not satisfied with his insistence that " it must be it," and went on asking " why ? " However, the argument satisfactorily over, keeping outside Dubh Sgeir we motored in to the small bay two hours before low water, the "dries eight-feet" rock being a useful guide.

TINKER'S HOLE. See photograph, page 59.

What a fascinating place this is ; a small land-locked natural anchorage, surrounded by rugged walls of red granite, with perfect shelter from all winds and swell and yet with a view over the Torranan Rocks as far as one can see. My wife was tremendously impressed with the beauty of the colours we have seen to-day; the whiteness of the Iona sands; the blueness of the sky ; the water deep blue, light blue and green, and the red granite rocks which look warm in the evening sunlight.

Erraid is, of course, also of interest to readers of Stevenson's *Kidnapped*, as it was here that David Balfour was marooned after the wreck of the brig *Covenant* on the Torranan Rocks.

Late in the evening we climbed up to the old tower used for signalling to Skerryvore and Dubh Artach (which was built of Erraid granite) and had a truly wonderful view " from Rum to Ireland."

Leaving next morning with the first of the flood, having passed the "dries eight-feet" rock at the entrance, we carried on almost as far as Dubh Sgeir before turning south-east to take the passage inside the Torranan Rocks. That is indeed a horrible collection of rocks scattered over an area of about ten square miles south of the Sound of Iona. Having seen Rankin's Rock (really two rocks) we passed close to the south side of Sgeir Calliach. We saw the Beacon on Ruadh Sgeir, the most easterly of the rocks, and about half-way between it and Eil. Chalman spotted the " dries four-feet " Bogha nan Ramfhear just awash, so took the passage between it and Eil. Chalman. After that there was no difficulty and we were soon past the prominent Ardalanish Point. In clear weather all this is plain sailing, even though its description may seem a trifle complicated, but in thick or dirty weather it must be both difficult and dangerous.

From the Ross of Mull to the Firth of Lorn, about thirty miles, there is no anchorage with the possible exception of Carsaig. We had a look at this pretty bay, but thought that there would be but little peace behind the islands in strong southerly winds. As a refuge it might be useful especially as there are rings on the two largest islands.

As there was no wind we motored slowly along admiring the fine basaltic cliffs, but off Loch Buy, getting a light southerly, shut off the engine and ran to Brandy Stone, where as already related, we were lucky in meeting *Fiara*.

LEAVES FROM ROWAN'S LOGS

Puillodobhrain to Loch Craignish

As I have already mentioned we always visited Puillodobhrain on our way home, and even when we were storm-
stayed here in 1931 for four days the time passed quickly.
There was a lot of dinghy sailing and John and Neill did much
" exploring " ; my wife did her usual big washing ashore ;
we all walked to Easdale, " had a huge lunch at the hotel, but
were able to walk back, getting soaked on the way " ; *Ripple*
(R.C.C.) was lying near us, and we saw a lot of Spiller and his
crew, a young New Zealander ; *Droleen*, in a great hurry to
get home, came in but was held up for two days by the gale ;
when they got away it was under a diminutive trysail, foresail
and engine.

We usually left in time to get the ebb past Fladda down
Scarba Sound, round Ardluing Point and then either inside
Ris an Vic Faden or between Corr-easar and Ris an Tru,
through the Dorus Mor and up to an anchorage in Loch
Craignish. (There is no trouble from Coirebhreacain on the
way south as one comes with the ebb.)

In 1932, however, we came with *Fiara* through Cuan Sound·
With a fair wind and at slack water (high water) we had no
difficulty with either the Cleit Rock or the telephone wire,
which at its lowest point seemed to be a good twenty feet
above our truck which is forty-four feet above the deck.
The note in the Pilot that it sags to within about fifty feet of
high water is definitely an under-statement.

Fearnoch, Loch Melfort

Running up Loch Melfort with *Fiara* we anchored in three
fathoms off the stone pier at the head of Fearnoch Loch, but
when the force of the south-west wind increased in the afternoon we both dragged, so shifted in closer to the west shore
and laid kedges. It poured all afternoon and by evening was
blowing very hard. We had missed the morning forecast,
which had foretold a gale from Mull of Galloway to Cape
Wrath, but we heard it at night. Neither McStay nor I was
greatly taken with this place as we could not get out of the
swell which was coming up the loch with the south-westerly.

Craobh, Loch Shuna

This is an anchorage completely sheltered by three small islands : Craobh, Dun and Buidhe, which may be very convenient if, having got through the Dorus Mor on the way north, or past Fladda on the way south, one is too late for the other. Although there is only one and a quarter fathoms in the south and a one-fathom patch in the north entrance it is easy to get in. There are one or two seven- to nine-fathom holes, but it is not difficult to find a spot with only four.

We came in here on our way south, in 1931, and Charlie and Bob walked over the hill to Ardfern for letters. Finding a grocer's cart there they arrived back heavily-laden with bread, jam and other things, and were very chagrined when, just as we were taking them hot and tired on board, the self-same cart turned up at the bay.

We came back here again the following year with the Robertsons, having come through the canal in company with *Gigha*. We left before them next morning, having advised them to take the Cuan Sound passage, and had a wet beat to Puillodobhrain. I have already related how, having found them again after ten days at Drumbuy, we heard of their misadventures.

* * *

On our arrival at Loch Craignish in 1930, after our short cruise to Drumbuy, we found that the Crinan Canal was closed. So, after lying there for a couple of days with *Deirdre*, we sailed with a light westerly to Tayvallich, Loch Swen, intending to leave my wife and the three youngest members of the crew there so that Charlie, Bob and I might feel less encumbered in the passage round "The Mull." We failed to find any accommodation for them there, but left them ashore next day having engaged a car to drive them to the nearest available lodging.

Gigulum Sound, Gigha

We had a fast run to Gigha, and, as I thought we might some day be thankful to know our way into Gigulum Sound from outside, we went down the west side of the island. We kept well off shore as it is foul, and after passing Cath Sgeir lightboat and Leam I., opened up the Sound. Then, at a most inopportune time we had a tremendous deluge of heavy rain which blotted out everything, and it was only after a very tricky bit of navigation by Charlie that we anchored south-west of the pier in three fathoms.

This is the most sheltered place in the Sound, or perhaps it would be better described as the least exposed, and is more or less out of the tide. It is located by two lines, the north peak of Gigulum just open south end of Oulsin I., and Gigulum Rock buoy showing clear of north end of Oulsin I. A third line which is useful is that the bollards on the pier in line clear the rocks to the south-west of it.

H. M. Wright in *Espanola* (R.C.C.) came in from the north soon after us, having had no little difficulty in negotiating the obstructions in Gigha Sound during the downpour. Later in the evening *Quest III* joined us, also on her way south.

It blew hard from the north during the night and I had some difficulty rowing " Billy " ashore in the morning, but when I asked Wright what he thought of the day, I was told " sure, it will take off."

To make sure of getting the first of the flood round " The Mull " we left at 9 a.m. under mizzen and jib, and soon were enjoying our first experience of a genuine Channel sea. But at 10.30 a.m. Charlie reported two disturbing facts, first, that there was a gale warning, force eight, from the Isle of Mull to Stranraer, direction north to north-east, and second, that Bob was in the cabin " reading Blackwood and looking very green."

In brilliant sunshine, taking no water on board and being followed by a well-behaved dinghy, we had a grand run at six knots to Deas Point which we passed dead on time. Following a drifter which was hugging the shore we dodged the " race," which we could see further out.

As we were now in quieter water, although the wind was as strong as ever, we had a quick hot lunch and we even washed out " Billy 's" bad eye as ordered by my wife. (He had come off second best in an encounter with a cat at Tobormory). Bob's complexion and spirits were now normal. *Quest III* had already passed us under trysail and jib bound for Belfast, and near Sanda *Espanola*, under heavily reefed mainsail and jib, overtook us. We noticed a yacht lying most uncomfortably north of Sanda, and a couple of lighters sheltering in Carskey Bay. I made a mental note that if we carried away anything we would always be able to run back and join them.

The sky was now overcast and the wind gale force, so we discussed whether we should hoist the trysail to give us more drive in what we knew would be a hard beat to Campbeltown. As we had previously had little satisfaction with this sail and some trouble with the lead of the sheets, we left it below and carried on with mizzen and jib.

Once round Dunnighn Point we felt the full force of the gale, and with the flood against it there was a nasty steep broken sea. We took short boards close inshore hoping, unsuccessfully, to get quieter water, and as we were having difficulty in staying put on the engine and changed to No. 2 jib. Neither the water nor the sky was any longer blue, but we had no idea of whether it was raining or not as there was a constant smother of water.

Off Davaar Island the squalls were exceptionally fierce and the sea very confused, and I was glad indeed when we had weathered it and had run into the bay cold and drenched to the skin. We had taken three very long hours from Arranman Barrels—only ten miles—but *Espanola*, who had taken a long board out towards Arran and who was carrying her dinghy on deck, got in only half an hour before us. So we felt we had done not so badly.

Campbeltown

Just before we opened out the bay we had seen *Molita* running down in fine style from the north and when we anchored ahead of her on the north side of the bay were surprised and delighted to be hailed by Wm. Sewell.

Everything had been so well stowed below that with the exception of the kettle, which had jumped off the stove, nothing had shifted. The only damage we had was a broken jib-sheet shackle and bulkhead mirror, neither of which was noticed until our arrival. I took "Billy" ashore and after telephoning various places found that the shore party were comfortably housed in Lochgilphead.

The day had been full of extraordinary contrasts. First there was the exhilarating run down the Sound of Jura, the water a light blue with white-crested waves which seemed to have been designed to suit our ship, and overhead a blue sky with a few small clouds racing south, the advance party of the main body. Next came the short stretch of quieter

73

water, but with no lessening of speed, in Sanda Sound with its interesting new landmarks. This was suddenly followed by the cold wet " slam-bang " to windward with the flood knocking up a vicious grey sea that seemed determined to beat us in our struggle against the northerly gale. And finally the feeling of relief when we got to windward of Davaar Island.

Now that is a long story, but if any one thinks that I have made too much of a song about this passage I would refer him to a very realistic article in the *Yachting Monthly* of July, 1931 by H. M. Wright entitled " Force 8."

Next day, although the gale signal cone on the pier was down, we preferred the comfort and companionship of our anchorage to a beat up Kilbrennan Sound. So we spent the day, and the next day too, yarning with Sewell, Wright and William McStay of *Fiara*. Wright was particularly interested in *Molita*, who was an older sister of *Espanola*, having been built in the same yard four years earlier.

Fiara was one of the hard sailed Irish yawls and McStay knew my wife's Belfast cousins very well, having often raced against them. Although *Fiara* has been mentioned several times already in this story this was the first time we had met the McStays. They followed us to Rhu, and after that and again in 1932, 1933 and 1934 when they cruised with us, we saw a lot of them. We lost a very good friend when McStay died in 1934.

Several other yachts came in including *Seagull*, whom we had seen at Sanda; *Rosemary*, in very bad shape, having had a hard passage from West Loch Tarbert, losing her dinghy off " The Mull " ; and others from the north, but none of these had made a passage on the day we came round. An interesting arrival was H. M. *Spey* escorting a Dutch trawler whom she had caught fishing off Ailsa Craig.

On the third morning we got away early hoping to make Rhu, but after a long slow beat we anchored for the night at Wood Farm Buoy, Kyles of Bute, getting a fair wind home next day.

During our cruise up north to South Rona in 1931 the weather had been very un-summery, but it was perfect when, leaving Craobh, Loch Shuna, we sailed down the Sound of Jura and up Loch Swen to Tayvallich. The Crinan Canal was available, but I wanted to come round " The Mull " again with the whole crew on board, but in quieter conditions than we had experienced the year before.

We ought to have pushed off next morning as although the glass was low it was steady, but Spiller, who had come in in *Ripple* soon after us, persuaded us to go with him to the Fairy Isles, in Sailean Mor. So we dallied there for a day, " sleeping, eating, swimming, dinghy-ing and full of confidence that summer had come at last."

We left next morning bound for Gigha after getting a forecast of west to north-west winds, moderate to fresh, and showers with bright intervals. Off Dana we got some heavy squalls, " several planks under, several lockers emptied," and when reefing carried away the topping lift. So we anchored, and while some of us remained on board to repair the damage the others visited the McGuigans, returning laden with chickens.

Getting away again under full sail we took the passage inside Eil. nan Leac as we could just lie it, to the consternation of the McGuigans who were watching us. As the wind freshened we had again to reef and when doing so the worm of the reefing gear carried away. This was something we could not repair, but dropping the mainsail we carried on with mizzen and jib. Conditions, however, steadily got worse, " wind increasing, sea rising, continuous rain and no sign of the promised bright intervals." When off Knap Point we gave it up and ran back in a downpour of rain to Tayvallich. We found Spiller a bit worried about us as it was by this time a very dirty day. Late in the evening, *Deerfoot*, a heavily built twenty-nine-ton ketch, came in from Campbeltown having had a very rough passage from Gigha.

If we had had ordinary reefing in addition to roller gear we would have gone on, but would probably have run into West Loch Tarbert. The evening forecast confirmed our opinion that the wind had been of gale force and in the circumstances we felt that we had been wise to have turned back.

We spent two more days at Tayvallich (Neill being in his bunk with some fever), and had welcome visits from Dr. Guy and family, Margaret Gray, and the McGuigans with more chickens. With a moderate westerly we then sailed to Loch Craignish looking for *Fiara* in vain. Hearing that she had passed through the Canal the day before we followed as fast as we could, but on arrival at Tarbert found that she had left for home. So we had had two disappointments, and as our cruise finished, summer arrived.

IX

1934 : Failure to get North

I WAS looking forward confidently to more extensive cruising this year and hoped by improving the yacht's windward work, her only weak point, that we would be less dependent on favourable winds. So McGruers put one ton of the lead internal ballast outside above the iron keel, which was dropped eight inches aft and six inches forward. Her new *draft* was 5 ft. 8 in. and the *water-line-length* was 28 ft. 6in.

Being now one of the unemployed I had more time at my disposal, but I soon found out that I was to have more difficulty in collecting my crew. Charlie, now a B.Sc., was a busy engineer at Yoker ; Bob was a final year medical student ; Mary was a nurse in Glasgow. I also failed to appreciate that these three besides being now rather big for their bunks had acquired an independence of character which made them, as I saw it, less amenable to reason.

The yacht was in the water sooner than usual, on April 4th, but fitting out was made very difficult by two weeks of very bad weather. So the year had started inauspiciously. When we were ready for sea and the weather had improved, I found that the attraction of the University dances was too strong for Bob, and that his sister was easily led astray by him. Then illness supervened. John was laid up in May, and Mary spent most of the month of June in bed when the weather was really very fine.

So it was July before we got away, my brother F.H.C. taking the place of Charlie and Bob who were to join us later.

When nearing Skate Island, Robertson (now owner of *Sylvia*) told me in passing that he had only with some difficulty got back through the Canal as the water was so low, and on our arrival at Ardrishaig we were informed that it was " temporarily closed." It was difficult to know what we should do. If I had had my full crew on board we would have gone down to Campbeltown without delay and, if the weather was suitable, have gone round " The Mull." But our arrangements were rather complicated; my brother was due to leave in a few days when A. McK., Mary's Spean Bridge friend, was to join us, and later Charlie, Bob and a friend, H.B. were also expected.

So we decided to wait about hoping that the Canal would re-open. We spent the next week in Loch Fyne at Tarbert, Loch Gair, Minard and Black Harbour, the overflow sleeping ashore in a tent. But as the weather remained good, in fact perfect, the Canal became drier and drier and the authorities at last said there was no hope. If only we had turned south a week earlier we would have had an easy passage round " The Mull " and by this time would have been well on our way up north. We were to pay dearly for our unfortunate delay.

All our visitors being now away and the full crew aboard we made for Campbeltown post-haste, or rather at six knots close-hauled. No sooner had we arrived there than the weather broke down. A forecast of a depression approaching from the Atlantic kept us there a day, and when we did set off next day we had got little south of Davaar Island before we got a forecast of " fresh to strong south to south-west winds, visibility deteriorating, further outlook, winds strong in the west." I decided that conditions were not favourable; but it was only after a bit of a breeze that I got my way, and turning back we ran with a couple of reefs down to Tarbert at seven knots. As there had now been heavy rain for two days I hoped that perhaps the Canal would have re-opened, but as this was not the case we carried on to *Loch Gair*.

* * *

So great was the feeling of disappointment and frustration on the part of the older members of the crew that a mutiny broke out, my wife, I regret to record, being the ring-leader. We ought to have stayed at Campbeltown; we ought to go back there at once, and so on. They took exception to my fondness for finding a snug anchorage fairly early in the evening, had queer ideas about the pleasures of sailing all night, scoffed at barometric changes and weather forecasts and held tidal streams in disrespect.

So a new Skipper having been appointed, we left Loch Gair late one afternoon and when trying to pass Otter Spit against the flood were hailed by R. Bruce Taylor, now in *Ulva*, whom we had seen at Tobormory in *Zaidie* in 1931.

When I asked him what should be done with a mutinous crew he shouted back " push them overboard and drown them." Failing to stem the tide, to my unconcealed satisfaction, the *Soviet* brought the ship back to Loch Gair, and when within a few hours it was blowing " good and proper " I think they were almost as glad as I was that we were not then beating down Kilbrennan Sound.

Two days later we returned to *Campbeltown*, more peacefully, to meet *Fiara*, and after a day there I resumed command with the moral support of McStay.

Leaving Cantyre behind us we had a fine run with *Fiara* to *Lamlash*, where we were storm-stayed for four days as the weather had gone all to bits. As Charlie had to get back to work we finally got off although the north-westerly was still strong and with two reefs down had a very wet sail until we got into quieter water past Garroch Head. It was now blowing gale force, and I remember my wife during a severe squall saying she hoped the keeper on the Cumbrae Lighthouse was watching us. Dropping the mainsail and carrying on with mizzen and jib seemed to me a surer guarantee of our survival.

We had no doubt to-day of the benefit of our increased draft, especially when close-hauled in the short breaking sea that the north-westerly kicked up against the flood. McStay, following us to Rhu, told me later that he had found mizzen and jib " almost too much."

We were back at Tarbert a week later and were glad to find *Fiara* still there, although sorry to notice that McStay was not well. In the afternoon *Vida VI* came in leading the fleet from Hunter's Quay by half an hour. In her somewhat old-fashioned rig of gaff-mainsail and jackyarder she crossed the line running before a fresh southerly on port gybe looking what she is, a fine ship. And then her veteran owner did a most extraordinary thing which made us gasp. Being rather short-handed he did not care to risk the gybe which would have taken him out of the bay and allowed him to take off some sail so, hauling his wind, he looked for a gap in the cluster of large yachts anchored there. Passing one after another he found no room to run up, so he deliberately ran his ship on to the small stretch of shingle just outside the black perch. When he had got that length his only alternative would have been to charge into the inner bay and that might have been disastrous. Happily he got off with the rising tide practically undamaged.

While we had a comfortable sail back to Rhu, McStay had a rough time before he reached Cultra, Belfast Lough, and took to his bed. He died at the end of that year.

Notwithstanding the limitation of our cruising this year and although there were some grumbles, agreements to differ and sometimes differences without agreement, there was lots of good fellowship and pleasure. It was really not so much that " crabbed age and youth cannot live together " as that " youth is full of pleasance, age is full of care."

At *Tarbert* we took full advantage of the exceptionally fine spell of weather ; there was lots of bathing in the outer bay, dinghy-sailing, varnishing of the top-sides and, of course, intercourse with our neighbours. Owing to the closure of the Crinan Canal there were always a lot of boats, and on one occasion the bay seemed to be full of Irishmen, *Espanola*, *Albatross VI* (Dr. Gunn), *Gannet* (Dr. Wilson), *Onora* and *Vaila*.

We spent perhaps too many days at Loch Gair, but it has many attractions and those who slept ashore found tent-life very pleasant, although once when Bob, evidently fed up with all this inactivity, deserted ship, " it rained *very* heavily." It was here that " Neill did his first oil painting and got himself into an awful mess." There were usually several other yachts here ; on one visit we found nine. We spent a cheery day with R. Bruce Taylor whose heavily-canvassed *Ulva* seemed a bit of a handful for him and his wife, but his spirits were as high as ever.

Minard Bay reminded us of Kintallen ; from here we visited the old Castle Lachlan on the other side of Loch Fyne. It had been a stronghold of the Clan MacLachlan whose fifteenth chieftain left here to fight and die at Culloden.

We did not care much for Campbeltown, probably because we did not get the weather we wanted there, and those who walked across to Macrihanish after we had decided not to move were too inclined to emphasize the quietness of the sea on the other side.

Nor did we enjoy Lamlash. It is too big a bay in which to be comfortably storm-stayed. On one really bad day, when we were lying to thirty-five fathoms chain, with an angel down as well, we could not get across to *Fiara* and two yachts beside us dragged badly. The young able-bodied members of both crews had a good day up Goat Fell, when the rest of us had a few hours peace. One extract from the log reads; " Charlie and Bob had tea on *Fiara*, arriving back after midnight and making far too much noise," so evidently it was time we were heading for home.

As it seemed improbable that we would be able to collect the family another year for cruising, and as *Rowan II* was larger than my wife and I required, we decided, but not without much regret, to sell her and to buy something more suitable. A proposal that a motor boat would be a more suitable craft for a couple who were nearer sixty than fifty, was turned down, and on the rebound we bought *Valdai*, a 1930 six-metre, from (the late) Robert Clark. *Bud* went with *Rowan II*, but we kept *Berry*.

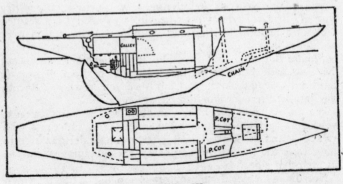

ROWAN III

L.O.A. 35ft. 6in. L.W.L. 22ft. Beam 6ft. 9ins. Tonnage T.M. 5 tons.

PART III

The Berries are Red—1935 to 1937

I

Rowan III. A 6-Metre Conversion

VALDAI was an international rating class six-metre, designed by Mylne and built in 1930 at Port Banna-tyne. She was bigger-bodied and had more generous freeboard than most of her class at that time and this was an important consideration in her conversion for cruising. Her principal measurements were : *length overall* 35 ft. 6 in. ; *water-line-length* 22 ft. ; *beam* 6 ft. 9 in. ; *draft* 5 ft. and T.M. 5 tons.

Her new name, *Rowan III*, seemed most appropriate for she had the kenspeckle red colour of all the Clarks' sixes, father's and son's.

McGruers of Clynder carried out some structural alterations which we hoped would give my wife and myself sufficient comfort when cruising and yet not prevent us occasionally joining the under seven-ton class in handicap racing.

The original small steering *cockpit* was enlarged to 4 ft. × 3 ft. and had deep coamings ; the large forward cockpit was covered by an inconspicuous coach-roof which had armour glass lights ; a small forehatch with deck light and deep wings was added.

The original *sail plan* was retained, but for cruising we had one of the three mainsails cut down from 365 to 300 sq. ft., a stout genoa jib cut down to make a trysail of 125 sq. ft. and three jibs 175, 120 and 45 sq. ft. The mainsail had ordinary reefing gear and all cruising canvas was tanned.

A strong removable iron crutch well over to the port side of the counter held the boom clear of the cockpit when at anchor, and a canvas cover over the boom kept rain out of the cabin.

Wishing to get rid of the bogey of foul anchors, usually nobody's fault, I was attracted by the advantages claimed for the *C.Q.R. Anchor*. Taylor suggested that one weighing 10 lbs. would be sufficient for so small a craft, but as this seemed too like a toy I chose one of 20 lbs. To keep the deck clear this was stowed in the fo'c'sle with 15 of the 30 fathoms ⅜-in. chain, the remaining 15 lying under the floor-boards just aft of the mast.

Five partial bulkheads were built in which, in addition to sub-dividing what had really looked like an empty shell, conserved the strength of deck and hull. In the *fo'c'sle* were fittings for two pipe cots, but the starboard one was usually left ashore and oilskins hung in its place. In the long cavernous space below the foredeck and forward of the samson post we stowed sails, etc. There was a small compartment on port between the fo'c'sle and cabin where we kept our clothes in kit bags. These had coat-hangers which, in addition to holding them up, kept their mouths open so that one could get at their contents very easily. Here also was kept the sanitary bucket, an enamelled pail with a removable mahogany rim, which could be used most conveniently under the fo'c'sle hatch.

In the *cabin* we had 5 ft. 3 in. headroom under the coach-roof and 3 ft. 3 in. sitting headroom above the settees which with 6 ft. × 2 ft. Dunlopillo mattresses made comfortable, if somewhat narrow, berths. Bedding was kept in strong covers and used as cushions during the day. Lockers at the forward ends of the settees held on port charts and books and on starboard a " Sloop " wireless set and various odds and ends.

Opening off the cabin and extending aft alongside the cockpit were two large lockers. In the starboard one was our crockery, cutlery, a bread tin, etc. The port one was our *galley ;* it held two Primus stoves (one gimballed) which when in use stood on the door of the locker. This folded down and being supported by a bracket made a steady shelf.

I fitted *electric lighting* in the cabin and fo'c'sle using large capacity dry cells.

With considerable ingenuity on McGruer's part a three-h.p. Stuart Turner two-stroke *engine* was tucked in below the cockpit with transmission through a centrifugal clutch to a Brunton's folding propeller on the starboard quarter. I made some lockers outboard of the engine for bo'swains' stores, etc., and the spare anchor, a 35-lb. Fisherman, was stowed there. In the counter there were a 2-gall. petroil tank, a 2-gall. spare petroil tin, two 3-gall. water tins, the lead, anchor light and right aft warps, ropes, etc.

II

Racing and Cruising, 1935

LUCKILY there was a spell of quiet weather for two weeks after I had brought *Rowan* round from the yard to our moorings, as arranging for the stowing of all the gear I have mentioned, especially the " etc.," took some time. Fitting lockers is not easy on a lively ship when afloat especially when there is so little space to work in and every inch of that space has to be used. It was not so much a fitting-out job as a tussle in fitting in all the gear we wanted to take with us for cruising, and in making sure that everything would stay put. The ingenuity shown by anything at all movable is astonishing. No matter how well lashed down, jammed in or even caged, they seem determined to get free to perform all manner of acrobatics.

Charlie, Neill and I then had a two days' trial cruise to Tarbert in quiet weather, and " passing everything not under power " decided that we now had a thoroughbred to look after. We also found that the tiny engine was easily handled and could give us five knots in smooth water.

Even though we were loaded up with cruising gear we could not resist the chance of having three races before we went north. So on May 24th my wife stepped on board for the first time and we went across to Hunter's Quay where we picked up Bob, now a Resident Surgeon at my old hospital in Glasgow.

There were only three in our class and we all crossed the line with the gun. We were knocked out of first place by a " 19/24 " to whom we were giving a generous handicap, but were quite pleased to get a second flag in our first race. I say " knocked out," for the " 19/24 " had bumped us badly at a mark and to our surprise had not given up. As it was our first race we did not protest, but made up our minds to beat her next day, and we did.

We lay at Rothesay that night off the ladies' bathing place, which was the recognized best anchorage here long before the costumes of the ladies were any attraction. It is fortunate that the holding is good as the bay is quite exposed to the east and north-east. It began to blow hard from the east in the early morning, and it was most uncomfortable. So we were glad when we got off, carrying full sail, and moved up to the starting line off Craigmore.

The third boat starting very late was never in the race, but all we wanted was to have it out with the " 19/24." Bob made a very bad start, but did well in the very hard, very wet beat to the Skelmorlie Bank Buoy. It was quite unlike any sailing my wife or I had experienced, and it seemed wrong to submit any boat and her gear to the punishment she was getting. Quite soon my wife reported that there was a lot of water in the cabin, but we were too busy getting to windward of our opponent to bother about that. However when she said that the mattresses were floating up the sides to the ceiling as we lay over something had to be done about it. As the discharge from the Vortex pump was well under water at the time I was afraid to use it, so we bailed out vigorously with the bucket, being frequently interrupted by Bob's requests that the jib should be hauled in another inch.

After rounding the buoy with a four-minute lead and one foot of water over the cabin floorboards, we soon pumped her dry on the run to the next mark. We steadily increased our lead and finished a good ten minutes ahead with all our gear intact and won our first 1st flag. Crossing over to the bay below Castle Toward we anchored, had tea, dried ourselves and then beat home to Rhu.

We had had a fine demonstration of what a six-metre would stand up to and the confidence we had gained was to stand us in good stead many times later on. My wife was most enthusiastic, and it was difficult to believe that one year ago when lying at Colintraive on a cold evening she had horrified us by declaring, " I am too old for cruising and prefer the garden."

The reason why we had taken so much water on board was partly because we had forgotten to plug the fairlead in the forehatch, but chiefly because after weeks of warm dry weather the topsides had opened up. A strong hatch cover cured the former and the wet summer that was to follow the latter.

For our third race Charlie and I crossed to Gourock where Bob joined us. We found that there were four ex six-metres and three " 19/24's " in our class. After varying fortunes in the light variable wind we were apparently out of the hunt when we rounded the Hunter's Quay mark for the last time. The others all went off on a board on starboard towards Strone, so we threw about at once and made for the finishing line at Gourock. Nursing her very carefully in the light northerly we were just able to lie the mark and our refusal when badly placed simply to follow the others paid us and we got another first flag.

* * *

Trial Cruise to Oban : June 3rd to 25th ; my wife and myself.

I tried in Part II to avoid repetition by combining our four family cruises in *Rowan II* into one narrative, and while there was some continuity along the coastline the extracts were often out of chronological order and in consequence rather disjointed. So I will now for the sake of variety adopt the more usual though monotonous day-by-day staccato method. *Rhu to Colintraive :* Monday, June 3rd.—Left Rhu this afternoon, only two days after our third race, without any further preparation except taking the racing sails ashore and bringing the cruising ones on board, and stocking up the larder ; took it as a compliment to my efficiency as a boatkeeper that my experienced housekeeper found nothing to criticize ; glass falling, also heavy rain ; wind north-east, fresh and very cold, with as much wind as we wanted, especially off Loch Striven, had a fast run, anchoring at Colintraive in less than three hours ; after dinner visited *Sonas* (J. G. Allan) just home from a cold cruise up north.

Colintraive : Tuesday, June 4th.—Slow getting to sleep last night as it was very cold and the north-east was " howling " ; a late breakfast ; had tea with the Russells who are busy getting *Eilidh* ready for a cruise to Norway ; to bed early and with more clothes than last night.

Colintraive to Ardrishaig : Wednesday, June 5th.—With a light north-easterly had a quiet run to Ardlamont and a slow beat to Ardrishaig.

Ardrishaig to Crinan : Thursday, June 6th.—Heavy showers and a fresh southerly ; found the absence of a reverse a bit worrying ; carried the C.Q.R. in the cockpit ; jib-sheet winches very useful in the locks.

Crinan to Ardfern : Friday, June 7th.—Heavy rain, glass falling, a poor forecast ; visited by Dr. Riddell (of *The Ketch*) ; ran round under mainsail to Ardfern ; wind southerly and fresh ; heard in evening news that *Endeavour* had been dismasted at Southend to-day.

Ardfern : Saturday, June 8th to Wednesday, June 12th.— My wife went home by bus and steamer for the week-end ; kept myself busy finishing various odds and ends ; saw a lot of three young Irish lads in *Florence*, an old " 19/24 " ; they were trying to patch an old mainsail and hoping the weather would moderate and allow them to get back to Belfast ; as arranged got dinner at Mrs. C.'s but had difficulty in doing justice to her hospitality which included six chops ; as her " big house " was let sat in the wee kitchen of her " but and ben," and as she had done some local nursing, entertained her with suitable tales of a surgeon's life in a city ; on my wife's return as the weather continued to be past talking about stayed where we were, well sheltered from the strong southerly by Iscan Island ; during the next three days walked a lot, had tea with the B.'s, supper with the M.'s, talked with the " General " and tried unsuccessfully to " contact " the grocer's cart.

Ardfern to Craobh, Loch Shuna : Thursday, June 13th.— Weather improving at last ; the C.Q.R. came out so easily and unexpectedly that I plunked down on the foredeck ; handling the chain was a messy job as it was thickly coated with mud ; when this was going on was hailed by the *Loch Shiel* making for the jetty and scolded for being in the fairway ; surely MacBraynes have not a monopoly of all the water as well as the trade of the West Highlands ; beat out of the loch in a fresh south-westerly under reefed mainsail and jib ; going through the Dorus Mor with the last of the flood got into a really nasty tide-rip and took three or four big " dollops " into the cockpit ; then a fast run to Craobh anchoring beside *Albatross VI* (built at Kiel in 1924) ; visited Dr. Gunn ; after dinner rowed to Arduaine and 'phoned home ; all well.

Craobh to Loch na Keal : Friday, June 14th.—Spent the forenoon on Buidhe Island, my wife sketching and then tearing up the result ; after lunch, wishing to try out the trysail, in a downpour of rain and a strong south-east squall ran round to

Loch na Keal anchoring in a hailstorm in five fathoms past the church on port.

Loch na Keal, Loch Melfort : Saturday, June 15th and Sunday, June 16th.—My wife off again to Rhu ; spent the day drying sails, clothes, and sluicing out the bilges to get rid of the Ardfern mud ; had dinner at the hotel, and met Mr. B., who asked if I was not " afraid to be out there all alone " ; sunshine next morning, a welcome change ; did a lot of varnishing and roped the leech of the mainsail at the cringle.

Loch na Keal to Ardinamir : Monday, June 17th.—As soon as my wife arrived lifted anchor and beat across to Luing ; anchored outside the small bay at Ardinamir ; explored the entrance in the dinghy ; sailed in at high water ; after dinner walked to Cullipool ; got a wonderfully beautiful view of Mull, Scarba and Jura in the setting sun ; 'phoned home ; all well. *Note on Ardinamir Bay.*—I had been advised to look for this small landlocked bay between the south end of Torsa and Luing, and it was well worth finding. The C.C.C. Journal is unduly cautious in its reference to it, stating that " it is a small pool with a narrow entrance which is further contracted by a rock in the middle of it ; greater depths are reported than shown on Chart No. 2476, but it is only suitable for yachts of shallow draft." The West of Scotland *Pilot* describes it as " a small and shallow cove," and the only soundings given on the chart are $\frac{1}{4}$, $\frac{1}{2}$ and 1 fathom.

These pronouncements do not do justice to this excellent anchorage which may be very convenient if one has missed the tide through Cuan Sound. Approaching the entrance one should keep well off the reef on the south-west shore until a patch of gravel is abeam ; then hug the shore to avoid a shallow bank, which dries one foot midway between Torsa and Luing. At the entrance itself there is in the middle a rocky patch and on port a rock just off the shore both of which dry five feet. Steer between these in the direction of a rough stone pier on the west side of the bay and anchor between it and Torsa. The position of these rocks, if covered, can easily be seen by the masses of seaweed on them.

At Low Water Spring tides there is a least depth of $1\frac{1}{2}$ fathoms on this line, and we have had no difficulty in entering or leaving at low water, although the long strands of seaweed may foul the propeller. One can get three, four or five fathoms over most of the bay although it shoals at the south-west and north-east sides, and several yachts could lie in it without undue crowding.

It is absolutely sheltered from all winds, and although there is a channel through to the " turbulent tidal torrent " of Cuan Sound, it is so narrow and shallow that the tidal stream, while keeping the pool from silting up, does not disturb one's peace.

In addition to its natural beauty and security another attraction for us was the friendship we formed with the MacLachlans at the farm who give a courteous and interested welcome to any wandering yachtsman. We seldom failed to spend at least one night here going north or returning home.

Ardinamir to Brandy Stone, Oban : Tuesday, June 18th.—
A quiet night and a lovely morning ; ignoring a depressing forecast left under engine three hours before low water ; sailed through Cuan Sound with a leading wind one hour before slack water ; were almost held at the Cleit Rock but managed to stem the stream ; (the tide sets through at seven knots Springs, making one and a half hours before low water and high water) ; off Easdale Point the wind backed and

Ardinamir Bay, Luing. Soundings in fathoms.

lightened so gave up our idea of Tobormory and beat up Kerrera Sound to Brandy Stone ; anchored in seven fathoms beside *Leonora*.

Brandy Stone to Puillodobhrain : Wednesday, June 19th.— As the tide at Cuan Sound was not suitable for a lazy start contented ourselves with beating in a squally southerly into Puillodobhrain where we found *Lady Bridgella* ; heavy rain and a fresh southerly in the afternoon.

Puillodobhrain : Thursday, June 20th.—A day of wind and rain.

Puillodobhrain to Ardinamir : Friday, June 21st.—The fresh southerly and driving mist of the morning cleared after lunch ; left under full sail ; off Sheep Island wind fell away altogether so motored through Easdale and Cuan Sounds to Ardinamir preceeded by *Lady Bridgella* ; there was quite a big swell off Easdale so took the opportunity of becoming more familiar with the entrance to this sheltered natural harbour ; although silted up so much that there is barely swinging room it might be a useful refuge some day.

Ardinamir to Craobh : Saturday, June 22nd.—As the tide at the Dorus Mor was inconveniently early, slept till 10 a.m. ; Hedderwick wanted to shift anchor so gave him a hand, but my dinghy painter got foul of his propeller ; left him hard at work trying to get the tangled mess off with a big saw and walked to Cullipool ; on my return found him in a state of collapse and finished off the job with the boathook ; (a brand new painter arrived at my house on Christmas Day, " A present from *Lady Bridgella* ") ; in the evening sailed across to Craobh followed by *Lady Bridgella* ; a wonderful sunset ; my wife sketching.

Craobh to Crinan : Sunday, June 23rd.—Both awake at 6 a.m. ; not a breath of wind ; " mopped " out of the bay silently so as not to disturb *Lady Bridgella* ; with a light north-westerly sailed through the Dorus Mor to Crinan.

Crinan to Colintraive : Monday, June 24th.—My wife anxious to get back to Rhu to-morrow afternoon ; left at 6.30 a.m. ; locked out at Ardrishaig at noon ; motored in an oily calm all the way to Colintraive ; the little engine, using an absurdly small amount of fuel, took us the twenty-five miles in seven hours at half throttle.

Colintraive to Rhu : Tuesday, June 25th.—Got out of my bunk at 5 a.m. and without dressing was slipping along quietly with a light westerly without wakening my wife, when we were struck by a succession of squalls ; overhead there was a big black revolving cloud and the wind was coming from all directions ; anchored ; dressed ; breakfasted ; with a reef down and with all sorts of wind in force and direction got out of the Kyles ; shaking out the reef beat to Rhu, arriving at 3 p.m. just in time for Neill's school prize-giving.

* * *

Having had no previous experience of racing we had been more than pleased with our initial success, but our pride was humbled when after our cruise we again joined the racing fleet.

Although we were well up at the finish when there was any weight in the wind, we failed to get a single flag in six starts in the Clyde Fortnight. This was partly due to the enormous amount of cruising gear we had on board, but chiefly because we were terribly foul and grudged the time necessary for slipping and cleaning.

I disgraced myself just after we had anchored at Hunter's Quay at the finish of one of these races by falling overboard. Wishing to veer out some more chain, I had taken it off the samson post and was pulling some more up from below when it jammed in the hatch fairlead. I jerked it violently ; it came ; I went. I was still holding on to the chain but it was now running out freely, so dropping it I swam the few strokes necessary and climbed on board as the rest of the crew came up to ask what all the row was about. I was wet but happy as I had lost neither my spectacles nor my dentures.

III

A Fair Week in Loch Fyne

CRUISE *in Loch Fyne :* July 7th to 15th.—My wife, Neill, " Jack " and myself.

Deciding that cruising, not racing, was our métier we went off with Neill and " Jack " for a short cruise up Loch Fyne. We had a slow passage in a light southerly to Wood Farm Buoy, and the following day a good south-westerly to Tarbert. " Jack " seemed to be as much at home as he had been in *Rowan II.* He was, however, rather surprised when lying comfortably on the mainsheets off Ardlamont to find himself overboard, but was promptly rescued by my wife.

We were wakened in good time next morning—at 5 a.m. and again at 7 a.m. by boys selling herrings—but we did not lift anchor, as with a fresh southerly there was quite a big sea running outside. It was a fine day and Neill walked over to the outer bay and bathed. On the way back he managed to lose not one but two bathing suits and a towel ! In the evening *Morna* came in from Campbeltown.

The glass which had been falling soon rose again and we had six days of perfect weather. With *Morna* we sailed to Loch Gair and spent the evening with them, playing Lexicon, eating far too many sweets and sampling their Irish whisky. When we left with them next morning we sailed round them to show them what a fine little ship we now had, and then drifted down the loch to Black Harbour. It was very warm and Neill enjoyed bathing off the yacht. Just after he had climbed back on board we saw a large basking shark quite near us.

It was very warm again next day when we sailed back to *Tarbert* to allow my wife to go home by steamer ; more bathing ; a curious evening forecast " wind light, strong later."

Charlie arrived by steamer next day and we got off at once with a fresh south-westerly. The recent hot weather had opened up our topsides and we took in a lot of water on the lee side. Passing many basking sharks at Ardlamont we ran up the West Kyle and anchored east of the Buttock of Bute. With variable light airs we sailed to Sandbank where we picked up a mooring, returning to Rhu the following day after eight days' perfect cruising weather. Why is it not always like this ?

Being keen to do well " on our home pitch " at the Gareloch Regatta on July 27th, we had the yacht slipped, cleaned and freshly anti-fouled. We had been on the move all summer and had seldom lain at our moorings in Rhu Bay for more than a few days, so were astonished to find how foul she was. Like " The Old Superb " she was " green as grass below " and it was no wonder we had had no success in the Clyde Fortnight.

Bob coming from Glasgow saw that it was blowing far too hard in the open Firth for any racing, so was rather surprised to find us on board with the full mainsail up and itching to get off. (Bob is not often actually late but he is never early !)

We had some hard squalls before we got through the narrows and arrived at Clynder just in time for our start. The wind in the Gareloch was westerly, fresh and squally, but of course there was no sea to speak of.

We led the five six-metres in our class across the line. At the first mark we gybed in a hard squall and, being laid flat, got almost out of control to the danger of two others astern of us. After that we drew ahead and early in the second round had overtaken the *Islanders* who had started ten minutes before us. Increasing our lead in hard conditions that suited us we finished well ahead of our class.

A week later Charlie, Bob and John at the beginning of their cruise got a second flag in the Hunter's Quay to Tarbert Race, so we had retrieved our lost reputation.

* * *

Charlie's Cruise to Loch Sunart : August 2nd to 18th.—Charlie, Bob, John and later a nephew, Pat.

The mutineers of last year deciding that if the old folk could cruise in an ex six-metre surely they could do so also, had the effrontery to commandeer her.

They left Rhu at 11.30 p.m. on Bob's arrival from Glasgow, and very nearly finished their cruise in the dark on the Green Isle off Rosneath Point. Their success next day when racing

ABOVE ARDINAMIR, LUING, SHOWING CUAN SOUND BEHIND TORSA BEG

DRIFTING DOWN LOCH FYNE (MY WIFE, NEILL AND " JACK ") IN 1935

CHARLIE, BOB AND JOHN IN *Rowan III*, LOCH SUNART

TARBERT, LOCH FYNE

A " Cist " at Craignish

Celtic Broch at Glenelg

The "Pool," Kyle Akin

Rowan III in Scalpay Sound

to Tarbert was partly due to going off on their own when not lying too well near the finish, a manœuvre which had paid us so well at Gourock.

They were away for a fortnight, but as they kept no log, I have, perhaps fortunately, no record of their exploits except that they had been aground in the early morning at Tarbert (although " the Bay was very quiet this year " !) ; that Bob had climbed the 49 ft. mast at Ardrishaig to clear the fouled burgee ; that they had been to Macnevan Island, Easdale, Oban (where Pat joined them), Dunstaffnage, Port an Dun, Loch Aline (where R. Bruce Taylor dried them in *Zuleika*), Tobormory, Loch Sunart, and came home by Puillodobhrain, Craobh, Crinan and Tarbert.

* * *

Although my wife and I had not got any further north than Oban we had had a good trial cruise in weather that was mostly very cold and wet, and often treacherous. There had been no gales, but the changes from light to fresh and strong winds had been frequent and sudden.

The way our handy little ship slipped along in a light air, or in none at all was a revelation to us, as also was the way she could stand up to strong winds even though she seemed to be taking them lying down. With the mainsail and trysail hoisting on a track and the jib hanking on to the forestay, handling the sails was easy even though the deck space was so limited. The jib-sheet winches, which had been moved aft, interrupted an otherwise clear deck, but their usefulness more than compensated for an occasional stubbed toe. We seldom had to reef, and when it blew really hard she handled perfectly under trysail.

She was of course lively, and in rough water very wet, but the forehatch cover was effective and only once, in the Dorus Mor, did we take any water into the cockpit. So our Vortex pump was rarely used except when in a fit of enthusiasm I cleaned out the bilges.

Anchoring gave us no trouble at all ; after a few fathoms of chain had been led through the fairlead in the forehatch coaming and over the stem the C.Q.R. could be dropped overboard quite carelessly. (As the fairlead was at the side of the hatch the chain was apt to foul as I found to my cost

when I fell overboard at Hunter's Quay.) In *Rowan II*, using a Fisherman we had had a foul anchor a dozen times in six years; that inconvenience was no longer possible as this anchor has neither stock nor protruding fluke.

The coachroof and cockpit coamings gave complete protection from wind and water to any one not actually steering, and when at anchor the canvas cockpit cover over the boom kept out the rain. So we had comfort below. Stowing was a fine art in which we took great pride. Cooking, except when at anchor or in very quiet weather, was difficult, but we were quite content with a cold lunch between a good breakfast and an even better dinner.

In our short cruise with Neill and " Jack " we did not feel overcrowded, perhaps because we had such fine, warm, quiet weather. The four who cruised later insisted that they had had lots of room and had been quite comfortable in spite of poor weather; but it must have been a tight fit. For comfort, three is the maximum, and if the other is the right person, especially if she is a good cook, two is undoubtedly the best company.

We found it difficult to combine cruising and racing. With all our cruising gear on board we were three and a half inches below our original racing marks and needed a hard wind to do well. Another disadvantage was that owing to the coach-roof conversion the working space for the crew was so restricted that even three seemed a crowd.

1936: More Racing and Cruising

ADORNED this year with a gold line on her rubbing strake, *Rowan III* was brought round to her moorings in the middle of April, and as usual there were many things to be attended to. With much inconvenience I unravelled the thirty fathoms of chain and re-painted the red, white, and blue markings on it at five fathom intervals. This was a messy job and I vowed that in future it would be done before she was in the water. During the next few weeks I enjoyed some single-handed sailing.

* * *

We repeated last year's experience by taking part in the opening race of the season, on May 22nd, and were again successful. My wife, my brother-in-law (R.E.W.) and I left Rhu with barely sufficient time to reach Hunter's Quay a few minutes before the start. Our only opponent was another ex six-metre and as there was no one else to watch we had an interesting duel in a moderate westerly.

Crossing the line on her weather we were able, in repeated cross-tacking, to sit on her along the Cowal shore, and drawing ahead won by three minutes. The wind had strengthened considerably, and there were quite a number of mishaps in the fleet, but we had no worry except when the jib sheets slipped in a hard squall and we nearly rammed the commodore at Rothesay.

* * *

Rhu to Colintraive : Wednesday, May 27th.—Taking advantage of a moderate easterly, heavily laden with gear and stores for a four-weeks' cruise, left Rhu and ran to Colintraive.
Colintraive to Tarbert : Thursday, May 28th.—A quiet night, a lovely morning, a steady glass ; a slow run to Ardlamont and then a wet beat to Tarbert ; the bay seemed to be full of boats fitting out including three of the R.C.C., *Ripple* (Spiller), *Nova* (Arkle) and *Widgeon* (Harvey).

Tarbert : Friday, May 29th.—Very cold last night ; was told that as usual I had not brought nearly enough blankets for myself, but thanks to heavy winter underwear, pyjamas of Jaegar's thickest, a Shetland wool pullover, two jerseys and stockings was quite happy ; had an interesting visit from Harvey in the evening and argued about C.Q.R.'s and other things.

Tarbert to Crinan : Saturday, May 30th.—Had a very wet beat to Ardrishaig in a hard northerly which, coming off snow-covered hills, was very cold ; the three-h.p. then had to work all out when taking us through the canal to Crinan.

Crinan : Sunday, May 31st.—*Sea Swallow* lying in the Bay ; Mrs. McGrigor Phillips came on board when we were at break-fast ; she sat under the cockpit cover while we finished in the cabin ; blowing hard, heavy rain ; waiting here to-day for letters and rigging-screw bolts.

Crinan to Macnevan Island : Monday, June 1st.—Still pouring so did not take the early tide through the Dorus Mor ; sailed round to Loch Craignish in the afternoon with *Blue Bird*, Balfour's very original craft ; Balfour and a friend had dinner with us and we talked till midnight ; he is keen to sail in company and will not believe that he would not be able to keep us in sight.

Macnevan Island to Ardinamir : Tuesday, June 2nd.—Through the Dorus Mor with the first of the flood ; when passing Ris an Vic Faden took bearings of the position of Hutcheson Rock, which has only one and a half fathoms over it at low water, intending to have a look at it ; forgot about it ; soon after saw a dark patch, probably seaweed, and realized that we were passing within a few yards of the rock ; beat up Shuna Sound and into Ardinamir ; spent the evening at the farm ; *Blue Bird* arrived later.

Ardinamir to Puillodobhrain : Wednesday, June 3rd.—As usual left too early for our tide, so anchored for an hour off Dog Castle ; my wife and " Jack " ashore inspecting the ruin ; close-hauled through Cuan Sound against the last of the ebb ; a fresh north-easterly outside ; two boards saw us past Dubh Sgeir ; getting to windward in this boat is a much quicker business than in *Rowan II*, and much wetter too, especially if tide is against wind ; my wife noticed, fortunately in time,

that the jib was tearing at the leech ; got thoroughly soaked taking it down ; able to lie Eil. Dun so decided on Puillodobhrain as likely to be more comfortable than Brandy Stone ; getting the forehatch cover off and the anchor and chain ready just before we bore away was a very wet job ; had my hands full as we ran in and anchored off the trap-dyke.

Blue Bird had followed us through Cuan Sound but had turned back into Easdale as she found conditions too rough off Sheep Island. It had been very cold when beating, as the hills were still covered with snow, but after a change of clothes and lots of hot soup, we were ready to go ashore and enjoy the sunshine.

We walked to Kilninver and went by bus to Oban to get letters and stores. Our return journey to Kilninver was most entertaining. It had been market day in Oban and by the afternoon most of the farmers did not know whether it was English or Gaelic they were speaking, and they spoke all the time and were constantly shaking hands. We saw a calf being carried in a sack by two small bandy-legged men, with its head sticking out and a most pitiable expression on its countenance. The bus filled up with all sorts in all conditions : sober, half-sober, farmers, women with children, a minister, a man who had lost his wife and his hens, and so on. Then the wife turned up and the husband was sent off to look for the hens which he had left somewhere. We finally started without him and were just leaving the town when he was heard and seen shouting and running after us with the sack full of hens. His attempted explanations to his wife after he had got on board quite drowned the squawking of the hens. We delivered various parcels on the way and picked up more passengers including a woman carrying a baby rolled up in a rug in her arms. Only when the baby made strange noises and the rug was unrolled did we discover that it was a cat !

The conductor was a genial sort of fellow who smiled even when he upset his cash bag, but the driver was cantankerous and thundered along, cutting corners, dashing down hills and very nearly ran full tilt into a party of tinkers with an old motor car. A great entertainment for 1s. 4d. return.

Puillodobhrain to Brandy Stone : Thursday, June 4th.—The cold north wind during the night did not worry us ; were

101

very snug below ; in the afternoon saw *Blue Bird* beating up the Sound, so followed and passing her anchored at Brandy Stone.

Brandy Stone to Tobormory : Friday, June 5th.—A light southerly to Duart Point and then a moderate south-westerly to Tobormory ; by evening it was blowing hard from the south.

Tobormory : Saturday, June 6th to Tuesday, June 9th.—Had a warning of a south-west gale this morning, our first this cruise ; breakfast on *Sea Swallow* who is lying near us ; later when she was ready to leave heavily reefed and her chain was up and down, noticed that it had picked up an old net and was completely stuck in the hawsepipe ; some time before the crew, toiling at the winch, realized why their work was so heavy and so ineffective.

In the evening (the late) Sir Thomas Dunlop's *Ariana* and John Douglas's fine " little steam yacht " *Cecilia* arrived ; *Cecilia* is only 188 tons, was built by Inglis of Glasgow in 1890 and still has her original engines : " Clyde built, ye ken " ; *Blue Bird* turned up later, having put into Loch Aline yesterday, and now agreed that sailing in company with us was impracticable.

I disgraced myself next day by letting the dinghy get adrift, but fortunately her absence was noticed before she had reached the Doirlinn Narrows for which she was heading. Neither in the bay nor on shore was any one visible at 3 p.m. this Sunday afternoon, so I hailed *Ariana* and a motor launch was manned very smartly and the wanderer brought back. Sir Thomas Dunlop, passing in his sailing dinghy later, asked us to dine with them, and we had a very pleasant evening on board his fine steam yacht. For this happy introduction we had the truant *Berry* to thank.

We had hoped to get out to Barra but the weather was too uncertain, so we took a busman's holiday and went there in MacBrayne's *Loch Earn*. We called at Coll, Tiree, Castlebay and Loch Boisdale and as it was thick and dirty outside were more comfortable than we would have been in *Rowan III*.

On our return next day we found *Cecilia* still in the Bay and *The Ketch* came in later. A salmon, or part of one, that we had bought on Saturday and was to have been eaten to-night will have to wait as we have been invited to dine on *Cecilia*.

This " steam yachting " is a new problem. These hospitable friends probably think, quite erroneously, that we are having a miserable, half-starved existence in this small boat in this poor weather. It is delightful indeed to meet them, and, especially for my wife, to eat a good meal that someone else has prepared, but my second and last collar is now a bit flabby !

Tobormory to Salen, Loch Sunart : Wednesday, June 10th.— It poured all day yesterday, but this morning is sunny and warm ; lifting anchor, and with it a large bit of net, got off with a light westerly for Loch Sunart ; *The Ketch*, which left at the same time, held us as far as Auliston Point, but we then drew ahead and had anchored in three fathoms off the tin boat-house at Salen long before she appeared in the bay ; they would not believe that we had not had our engine on.

In the afternoon Dr. Riddell rowed in and asked us to dine with them ; this hospitality is really embarrassing ; will have to bring more collars another cruise ; had heard that Charlie was ill at Aberfoyle so phoned, and getting a good report enjoyed our evening on *The Ketch* all the more.

A beautiful evening, warm, dead calm when we rowed back, but as the glass was falling when we turned in I veered out chain to eighteen fathoms.

Salen : Thursday, June 11th.—Wakened at 5 a.m. as a strong southerly which had sprung up was bringing quite a big sea into the bay ; were tailing off rather near the west shore, so laid a kedge far out ; asleep again within half an hour ; blowing straight into the anchorage this morning but did not shift, as it was very wet and we were holding ; in the evening the wind dropped ; had a visit from a member of the Geological Department, Dundee, who was living in a tent on the shore ; he and my wife talked at great length about vitrified forts, etc.

Salen to The Gut, Oronsay : Friday, June 12th.—Sailed with a moderate north-westerly to The Gut ; entering at high water did not identify the rocky patch at the opening of the channel between the islet on port and Oronsay ; too close at low water, so moved further up ; the best spot is in two fathoms just past the corner of the islet, but before one can see between it and Oronsay ; this clears the rocky patch, which is shown on Chart 3185 (Loch Sunart) as a tiny speck, and gives ample swinging room.

Walked over to see if there were any yachts in Drumbuy but saw none ; later my wife walked across to see the Grahams at Dorlinn, crossing at low water ; in the evening walked all over the west part of the island and had a wonderful view.

The Gut to Loch Aline : Saturday, June 13th.—Ran across to Tobormory for letters and stores and then down the Sound of Mull to Loch Aline ; my wife then walked round the loch and after dinner both walked to Ardtornish Castle ; no other yachts anywhere ; blowing hard when we turned in (we had missed a gale warning) so my wife suggested that it would be more convenient to lay the kedge then instead of in the middle of the night as at Salen ; no kedge laid as we have lots of room and can veer out as much chain as required.

* * *

Loch Aline : Sunday, June 14th.—Got the gale warning, and the gale too, this morning ; raining very heavily ; here we stay.
Loch Aline to Shuna Cove, Loch Linnhe : Monday, June 15th.— The glass at its lowest this cruise but the sun shining ; motored out against the flood ; drifted to Barony Point ; then a fast run before a rising south-westerly getting a strong squall as we hauled round the north end of Shuna ; anchored beside *Jane*, east of Knap Point.

Sir Alex. MacCormick's *Frea* (R.C.C.) was in the bay ; he is a great friend of my brother H.S.C. in Sydney, and for this and other reasons have wanted to meet him ; torrents of rain ; walked to Appin and phoned home ; all well now ; decided not to disturb *Frea* to-night.

Shuna Cove : Tuesday, June 16th.—Hearing *Frea's* engine early this morning jumped into the dinghy, but was too late, so once more have missed Sir Alex. MacCormick ; heavy rain, but two tinkers on the shore assure us that they keep quite dry ; they have three dogs, each in a separate little tent ; bought a fine sea trout from an old fisherman, who having laid his net across the bay, spent the whole day chasing a seal away from it.

Shuna Cove to Camus na Gall, Lochaber : Wednesday, June 17th.—Glass rising at last ; ran with reaching jib as spinnaker through the Corran Narrows, noting the strong eddy on the Corran side, and anchored off the fence at Camus na Gall ; warm sunshine ; everything out to dry.

THE BERRIES ARE RED—1935-1937

Camus na Gall to Corrybeg, Loch Eil : Thursday, June 18th.—
A beautiful sunrise over the hills north of Ben Nevis at 4 a.m. ;
beat with the flood through the Annat Narrows into Loch
Eil ; anchored off Corrybeg ; walked two miles to the Post
Office but found it had " no telephonic facilities."

Corrybeg to Port an Dun, Loch Leven : Friday, June 19th.—
Left early to get the *first* of the ebb through the Narrows ;
" Why do we always have to get the first of the ebb or flood?" ;
found at Corran that the flood had started a quarter of an hour
instead of one hour after low water as stated in the C.C.C.
Journal and the *Pilot ;* beat through Peter Straits and anchored
in the inner bay at Port an Dun ; very fiery in the evening
with easterly squalls ; the two ferry boats moor here, so very
little room ; slipped down an angel.

Port an Dun : Saturday, June 20th and Sunday, June 21st.—
Hailed by the Onich cart when at breakfast so bought some
stores ; dinner at the Loch Leven Hotel ; in the evening heeling
over with the weight of the squalls ; (several yachts dismasted
to-day at the Royal Northern Regatta at Rothesay) ; next day
still very squally but warm and sunny ; ashore sketching
and reading.

Port an Dun to Dunstaffnage : Monday, June 22nd.—Very
hot ; lifted anchor ; my wife at the tiller found it difficult
not to charge up on the weather shore in a squall before getting
clear ; through the Peter Straits with a squally easterly and,
of course, with the first of the ebb ; gybed off the jetty, ran
past Kintallen and Shuna, down the Lynn of Lorn and then
close-hauled against the last of the ebb into Dunstaffnage,
my wife still at the tiller.

After lunch set off by road for Oban ; missed the bus ;
walking, " terribly, awfully hot " ; got a very welcome lift
from a man dead tired and almost asleep on his way home
from Wick.

Dunstaffnage : Tuesday, June 23rd.—Very hot ; rowed almost
to Connel Bridge ; 'phoned Charlie ; arranged to meet him
at Oban on the 26th.

Dunstaffnage to Puillodobhrain : Wednesday, June 24th.—
Beat to Oban ; got stores and papers ; anchored for two hours
at Little Horse Shoe Bay ; bought two lobsters while my wife
walked to Gylen Castle.

This ruin, most beautifully situated on a rock at the south end of Kerrera, was originally a Norse fortress. It was later one of the strongholds of the MacDougalls, and in it was preserved the famous Brooch of Lorn. In 1647 the Castle was taken by the Campbells, but the brooch was given back in 1826 by a Campbell to the MacDougalls and is now at Dunollie Castle, whose ivy-covered ruin stands at the northern entrance to Oban Bay. A fast beat to Puillodobhrain.

Puillodobhrain : Thursday, June 25th.—Dense mist; flat calm; in preparation for handing over the boat to the " Soviet " next day " thorough cleaned the cabin, washed out the bilges, varnished mahogany deckwork, etc." *Nirvana*, a nine-ton ketch built at Arklow, came in; her owner, Mrs. Crimmins of Cork, sails alone with " Mike," an Irish hand with a divil of a brogue.

Puillodobhrain to Brandy Stone : Friday, June 26th.—*Nirvana* left for Colonsay in dense mist; we ran with a light southerly to Brandy Stone, and after filling up with all manner of stores handed over to Charlie, R.S. and A.C.

The weather at the beginning of this cruise had been fairly good; the winds had been cold but never more than " fresh "; rain had been frequent but not continuous. But when we got to Tobormory we found conditions outside too bad for us; there were gale warnings both before we went to Barra in the *M.V. Loch Earn* and after we came back, and the rain came down in torrents.

Had there been any sign of the weather settling we would have gone on after our three days in Loch Sunart, but the glass went down steadily and reached its lowest when we had turned south and were having another gale at Loch Aline. It was only after we had returned to Loch Linnhe that it began to rise, and although it was a little exasperating to get this fine spell too late for our original plans, we enjoyed it to the full.

We had been fortunate in our anchorages; the laying of kedges at Salen and Port an Dun was not due to any fear of dragging, and of course we had had no foul anchors. We were glad to have seen old friends and had made some new ones, but the blank caused by McStay's death was not filled.

Charlie's Cruise to Loch Sunart : June 26th to July 12th.— Charlie and two friends, R.S. and A.C.

They kept no log and all they told me, at first, was that they had been at Shuna, Camus na Gall, Port an Dun, Loch Aline, Tobormory, Drumbuy, Salen, The Gut, Dunstaffnage, Oban, Ardinamir, Craobh, Ardfern and Crinan, where they left the boat.

When I discovered a large patch on the mainsail they confessed to having torn it when reefing in an unexpected squall at Corran, and a well-executed repair to the cockpit floor showed that somebody had been very heavy-footed. But the most amusing incident they related was the mess they got into at Easdale. Running in before a fresh north-westerly they anchored and very quickly had the mainsail down and stowed. They then found they were on the shingle; they insist that the C.Q.R. had dragged, but I refuse to believe it. R.S. jumping ashore tried to push her off; Charlie doing his best with the short boathook fell overboard. He had previously started the engine, so there was poor *Rowan III* now afloat with no one on board (A.C. had left at Tobormory) with the anchor down and the engine running ahead. After this exhibition of seamanship before a group of spectators on the shore, they cleared out and went on to Ardinamir.

* * *

A Cruise which was cut short almost before it had begun.

On July 17th Charlie and I motored from Rhu to Crinan where the boat was lying and sailed round to *Ardfern* for the night. We came back next day in dense mist and, to cheat the tide, cut between the south end of Macaskan and Liath sgeir More and inside Rabbit Island. We found *Failte II* (R.C.C.) at *Crinan Harbour*, her owner a long-passage devotee like Mrs. Crimmins. I suggested several good anchorages up the coast, but, having just had a long passage north, he set off next day for the long passage home to Wicklow.

Charlie had then to go back to his work, but my brother, F.H.C. and Bill, one of his sons, joined me. After a couple of fine days at *Ardfern* and *Ardinamir* we crossed to *Craobh* to drop Bill and pick up Neill. Rowing to Arduaine I heard by 'phone that Neill was ill, so our long planned cruise was off. The glass was steady and the sun shining, but the morning forecast had predicted " strong south-east winds "; as we were both now anxious to get home we decided to move on to *Crinan* without delay. We motored there in an oily calm, but there were big black clouds high overhead hurrying north. These did not spoil our pleasure in consuming on the way a chicken, which the farmer's wife had cooked for us, large quantities of potatoes, biscuits, scones, cheese and beer.

By next morning there was a south-east gale, due to " an intense disturbance," and we were glad that we were not lying inconveniently storm-stayed at Craobh. The following day we managed with difficulty to get back to *Ardrishaig*, but the gale showing no signs of abating we went back to Rhu by steamer.

My wife and I came back a few days later with Neill when he had more or less recovered, and after a night at *Tarbert*, had a fast run, thirty-four miles in six hours, with all the wind we wanted to Rhu. As Neill was not too fit he stayed below and my wife read *Skeletta* aloud until they were both hysterical.

* * *

In practically no wind at all we got a second flag at the Helensburgh Regatta on August 15th, and at Gourock on August 22nd we ran away from the other six boats in a moderate westerly and won comfortably.

At Hunter's Quay with my wife, John and Neill as crew we had a very interesting race on August 29th in a moderate southerly. Crossing the line just ahead of *Selene* and under her lee-bow I was so taken up with holding her that I almost forgot about the other four. After a ding-dong race we were lying second last with two legs to go, but as the wind increased we passed two boats on the beat from Kilcreggan to Gourock and got on to *Suilven's* tail on the run back to Hunter's Quay. I managed to get an overlap just as we reached the mark and he had to give me room as we bore away round it. As the line was oblique I thought that I had failed to get my bow in front, but from the Commodore a bit of red was seen ahead and we beat him by a split second, getting a second flag.

The handicapping for this race was exceptionally good as is shown by the corrected times : 2.49.58 ; 2.52.18 ; 2.52.18½ ; 2.52.20 ; 2.52.31 ; and 2.53.50.

In our four races this year we had got four flags : two firsts and two seconds, and I think that split-second win was the best of the four.

V

1937:

To Loch Torridon in Bad Weather

AS both the mainsail and working jib which we had used for two years' cruising were rather light and both were the worse for wear, we cut down the racing mainsail from 360 sq. ft. to 300 sq. ft. and replaced the old jib by a heavier one of the same size, 120 sq. ft. As neither of these sails was tanned we had now to carry a mainsail cover. We had also with us the old tanned reaching jib of 175 sq. ft. and the storm jib of 45 sq. ft.

Three feet six inches were cut off the mast as it was neither wise nor sightly to have it higher than was necessary, and 1 ft. 6 in. came off the boom. The result of this was, of course, that we would have to depend even more than before on a good breeze of wind for any success in racing, but that was a secondary consideration.

Our 20-lb. C.Q.R. anchor had never let us down, but with the chance of less sheltered anchorages in the more extended cruising we were hoping for, I replaced it by one of 35 lbs.

* * *

Cruise to Loch Torridon : May 24th to July 21st.—My wife, " Jack " and myself, and later Charlie.

In this cruise we were at a good many of our old anchorages, so to save repetition I will not give day by day extracts from the log, but will try to give a more general impression of our wanderings.

The outstanding feature was the weather; it was almost unspeakably bad. Byron, referring to England, " England, with all thy faults I love thee still," added, " That is, I like two months of every year." Had he been thinking of Scotland he would probably have said one month or even less. The west coast of Scotland is a perfect cruising ground and if only one could be sure of one month of fine weather it would be in Para Handy's words " chust sublime." The last three summers had been disappointing, but this year it was the worst ever.

It was fair when we left Rhu but steadily degenerated, and when we passed through the big gate of the sea-lock at *Crinan* a southerly gale was on the way.

We lay at *Ardfern* for five days on three of which we had gale warnings, and although it did not actually rain all the time the frequent showers were very heavy.

We went by MacBrayne's bus from the cross-roads to Kilmartin one day, and from there by hired car to Duntroon. Passing behind this fine old castle, which is still used as a residence, we came to the ruin at Ardifuir. This is a large circular fort, twenty-five yards across, which dates back to about 100 B.C. In the ten-feet thick wall was a guard cell on the right of the entrance, and a stairway on the left led up perhaps to a parapet.

On the way back we left the car at the north lodge of Poltalloch and my wife showed me the stone " cist " which she and Bob had inspected some years before when on a walking tour. When they were peering with reverential awe under the stone lid something moved. After accustoming their eyes to the darkness they realized with astonishment and relief that it was only a hen sitting on eggs which she had hidden there. " This narrow cell was life's retreat." As the hen would have had great difficulty in getting her chickens out of the 2½-ft. high stone chamber the lodgekeeper's wife was delighted to hear of her whereabouts.

Many similar cists have been found in the estate along this ridge, some containing urns, necklaces, etc., but no others with livestock. They are about three to four feet long, two feet wide, formed by four stone slabs for sides and one for the top. They may contain one doubled-up skeleton but sometimes an infant's as well.

In addition to these " short cists " there are several collective tombs or " cairns " in the valley below Kilmartin, four of which have been excavated and are now protected by the Royal Commission on Ancient and Historical Monuments of Scotland. These are stone chambers built above ground level and covered by large cairns of stones.

There are also in this neighbourhood several stone circles, standing stones and stones with cup and ring markings, which

CIST. See photograph, page 95.

like the other relics of prehistoric peoples date back to the Stone and Bronze Ages.

Another interesting, but not nearly so ancient feature is the small hill Dunadd which rises out of the "Great Moss" between Kilmartin and the Crinan Canal. It is supposed to have been the spot where the Kings of Dalriada were crowned.

Another day after seeing the beautiful gardens at Craignish Castle we were shown a mound near the entrance in which three cists had been uncovered by the roadman when getting sand for the road. Two beakers and a stone axe-head found in them had been sent to the National Museum of Antiquities in Edinburgh. In one of them I found several bones from which I knew that at least one of the bodies had been that of a child. (When re-visiting this place in 1939 we found that more cists had been uncovered, but unfortunately they had collapsed.)

When walking past a cottage near the head of the loch we spoke to the owner and complimented him on the beautiful garden he had made out of the rough hillside. He was a retired schoolmaster and many years before had been at Glasgow University with one of my brothers.

On the fifth day of our enforced stay we wandered up a path from Ardfern village which took us up a lonely little glen, past a lochan with the imposing name of L. Mhic Mhairten, to Barachan where we had a grand view of Scarba and Jura. We had a long talk with the farmer's wife who was busy baking, and when we left her kitchen she gave us some scones for which no payment could be offered. The children from this and a neighbouring farm must have a lonely walk, especially in winter, over the moor before they reach the road that skirts Loch Craignish.

Having seen where we wanted to go we determined to get off next day even if we had a gale warning at night. We had the warning, but we were lucky as, leaving very early to catch the tide, we had a quiet sail to *Ardinamir* and a pleasant afternoon ashore at the farm before the wind got up and "buckets" of rain came down. We were storm-stayed there for three days; the glass tumbled down and it rained and rained "torrents of rain," a "deluge." One day I walked to the "road end" in a downpour and asked a bus passenger going to Oban by Cuan Ferry to bring back letters and papers. In the afternoon my wife set off to meet the returning bus; it was an hour late; she went in it to Cullipool to do some " shopping " for five minutes; although the shop was closed she got in by the back door but all she managed to buy was a " week-old loaf "; then the bus tried to tow a disabled car back; the tow rope broke eight times before she left at the road-end; she came back in triumph absolutely soaked but with a loaf and a *Glasgow Herald*.

As my oilskins were now useless, and I do not blame Paisleys, Ltd., we were keen to get to Oban. We had a 7½-knot run in a deluge of rain before a rising southerly to *Puillodobhrain*. After a visit by bus to Oban, where we got not only new oilskins but two " chance baths " at the Station Hotel, we got back to find to our surprise that it was a fine evening. This improvement was short lived as next day, after a pleasant run with the reaching jib drawing well to Tobormory, the rain again descended and the strong southerly again arose.

So at *Tobormory* we stayed for three wet blustery days. Two men who had come across from Muck in a big motor boat for stores told me that it was " a bit fresh outside," and a fisherman said " the outlook isn't patent and you'd be better at Drumbuy than outside." My wife was really too energetic; I expect she was restless and disappointed that there were no cists to investigate; the ship was " spring-cleaned " every day and " big washings " were frequent. We had dinner at the Western Isles Hotel with (the late) Dr. and Mrs. Brown Kelly who took pity on us thinking that we must be utterly uncomfortable. We got a big batch of letters from the family including one from Neill in which he wrote that he had had his fourteenth beating this term, this time by the Head!

We slipped across to Drumbuy in a quiet spell, which was, however, followed next day by a gale. To compensate for this we had the cheery company of Robin Workman and three fellow Merchistonians on *Mavourneen*. They had found Salen so uncomfortable that they had come round under trysail for shelter. It was interesting watching them looking for a good anchorage as we were at the time on the top of the hill and saw how they nearly ran aground on the shoal. We had anchored in the small bay in the south-west corner and

Opposite : KENMORE, LOCH TORRIDON.

did not appreciate the C.C.C. Journal's recommendation as we could not get less than six fathoms and were in the tide. We also lost what sun there was very early as we were over-shadowed by the hill.

Knowing that a nephew, A.J.H.C. was expecting to arrive in a Destroyer, we went back to *Tobormory*. Four destroyers came in just before midnight, and finding a lot of boats in the bay, spent a long time anchoring and re-anchoring before they got what they wanted. It reminded us of the way " Jack " fidgets about with his cushion before he settles down for the night ! We spent the next forenoon on his ship and then set off for the north.

We carried a moderate southerly as far as Mallaig, but although it was long past dinner time we had no difficulty in resisting the temptation to go into that harbour, and with a failing wind found a new anchorage in *Inverie Bay, Loch Nevis*. Having entered the loch we passed Bogha Don on port and were then rather puzzled about Sgeir Dearg. The C.C.C. Journal describes it as " the extremity of a rocky ledge which extends from the shore." This is not correct. As is clearly shown on Chart 2496 (Sleat Sound) there is lots of water inside it, so keeping it to starboard we anchored in four fathoms off the shooting lodge. Although Inverie is on the mainland it is as isolated as an island. The road round the bay leads to nowhere ; mails and stores come from Mallaig by motor boat thrice weekly. The Bay itself is a large open bight, but where we were is sheltered and in this and other respects is infinitely preferable to Mallaig.

Having had our fill of strong winds and heavy rain we feel hopeful that fine weather has come at last. We had a fast run to *Isle Ornsay* where we lay for a night and then on to *Totaig, Loch Duich*.

We were too early for the flood at Kyle Rhea so anchored for a few hours at the mouth of Glenbeg River a mile south of Glenelg, and going ashore walked a couple of miles up the glen to see the brochs. We found it very warm ashore and were quite glad when we came to the first of the two brochs.

This is a fine specimen of these circular towers, built of undressed stones without any binding material, of which there are some 400 in the northern half of Scotland. The

BROCH. See photograph, page 95.

massive walls are double, tied together by horizontal slabs, the inner one being vertical, the outer one sloping in as it rises to about forty feet. The central court, usually thirty to forty feet in diameter, is open to the sky and the only external opening is the doorway. This is a narrow passage which widens from the three-feet at its entrance to about five feet at the inside. From it at one side is an opening into a guard cell and from the other side a stone stairway leads up to galleries and chambers within the thickness of the enclosing double wall.

From their position, usually in the valleys, they seem to have been used for the protection of the people of the soil and their cattle and stores. From the relics found in them it seems probable that they were erected by the Celts in the first century A.D., and were used for about five centuries.

In this Glenelg one only about half the original circle remains and its height is only thirty feet. It is believed that some seven feet of its height were used in the construction in 1722 of the neighbouring Bernera Barracks reminiscent of the unhappy '45. The internal diameter at the foot is about eleven yards and the double wall is eleven feet thick. Three galleries can still be seen, but the stairway is no longer there. The second broch, about one mile further up the valley, is similar but more dilapidated.

We were very pleased when, the day after we reached *Totaig*, the Robertsons appeared in *Eala* and entertained us with a tale of misfortunes. We had seen them four days before off Tobormory bound for Eigg. They had looked in at Kilchoan to give some friends a sail (a foolish thing to do when cruising !) and when lifting anchor had paid off on the wrong tack and crashed into a " puffer " lying beside them. Robertson was on the bowsprit when it carried away and did a flying trapeze stunt back on to the foredeck. The mainsheet then fouled the puffer and parted, so they had now to deal with a bowsprit alongside and a boom lashing about in a squall of wind. Some blood was spilt but no one was seriously hurt. Running back to Oban they got a new bowsprit fitted in record time, with the help of much tact and some beer, and resumed their journey north.

We had a gale warning the morning they arrived and thought that we had been lucky in having had three days of light southerly winds from Tobormory, but it was merely a reminder that even in mid-June we should not count on getting settled weather. For we now had quite a long spell—ten days—of good weather with only one day of heavy rain. The wind varied from light to strong and was from the north, but as we had no long passages to make we did not grumble.

Coming from near Loch Long, Firth of Clyde, we thought we would like to explore the other *Loch Long*. There was no wind, so we went up under engine. Apart from the bank at Cleasaiche there is no difficulty especially going up at half flood as we did. At the head of the loch off the clachan of *Sallachy*, when passing *Janetha IV*, I spoke to the skipper and casually asked him how his moorings were laid as I did not wish to foul them. So when he shouted "let her go," I had to obey and dropped the C.Q.R. in seven fathoms. When he saw me taking the lead he shouted across, "you've plenty water there"; I had, and plenty of chain out too! I am perhaps too inclined to invite local advice, and when it is given too polite to refuse it. The best spot to anchor is at the "I" of Fig Island on Chart 2676 (Loch Alsh and Loch Duich) in three fathoms.

VI

Three Mistakes

DURING this period of ten days fair weather, we made three very careless mistakes and as confession is good for the soul, I will describe them in detail.

The first was when, after a fast sail with a squally northerly to *Kyle Akin*, we went into the "*Pool*" south of the jetty. There is only half fathom at low water on the bar, so we arranged to go in at one hour before high water, and I intended using the end of the jetty as a guide. I stupidly did not realise that the jetty would be at least partly covered, and as there is no perch on it my calculation was useless. As a matter of fact we must have passed right over the rocks just outside the end of the jetty, but fortunately did not touch.

From the fishermen ashore I later got a very useful line; keep the east chimney of the last (white) house in line with a telegraph pole on the hill behind it until the jetty is in line, and then bear to starboard. A useful indication of the depth is that when the end of the Ferry Pier at Kyle of Loch Alsh is just showing there is one fathom over the bar.

This Pool or Basin is small and we had difficulty in finding room beside the fishing skiffs, motor boats and moorings for the three ferry boats, so at the invitation of her owner tied up alongside the *Cutty Sark*. This skiff is owned by a Banffshire man who still has his East Coast accent although he has been here for many years. From him and his sons, and indeed from all the fishermen here, we got nothing but kindness, and when we left it was with a promise, which we fulfilled, to come back again. They had recently had poor fishing and their nets were badly torn, but instead of grumbling they spent the whole day mending them and had no time to read the papers we gave them. They were interested and surprised at the amount of comfort we had below, and, although they must have thought ours a very unsuitable boat for these waters, the only criticism they allowed themselves to make was about our low free-board.

With our newly acquired knowledge we sailed out two days later at two and a half hours flood, and had all

THE " POOL." See photograph, page 96.

the wind we wanted (northerly) and quite a jabble of sea up the Inner Sound and round the north end of Scalpay. After that it was a run in quiet water to a beautiful anchorage at the north end of *Scalpay Sound*. We lay just inside a sandy point off a lonely cottage where, after dinner, we got milk and eggs from a woman who had very little English, but whose courteous manner is typical of the West Highlanders. Later we rowed to the narrows and I made a note, for use perhaps some other time, that when the guys on the perch are covered there is at least two fathoms in the channel.

Nothing could have been more beautiful than the view up Lochs Ainort and Sligachan when we passed them next day on our way to *Portree*, where we arrived thoroughly soaked after a wet beat from Raasay Narrows. Soon after we had anchored we saw a really funny exhibition of bad seamanship by a yacht of about twenty tons with two ladies, two men and two paid hands on board. They anchored first of all just inside Sgeir Mor and stowed their sails. Then lifting anchor they motored round the bay, here, there and everywhere, finally anchoring too close to another yacht. This was not final as they were asked to move, so under engine again they resumed their wanderings until the engine stopped. After some time this was re-started, and after another tour they anchored this time for good and to everyone's relief far out. And she was a fine ship.

From here next day in a light northerly we beat to *Acarsaid Mor* and that was where we made our second mistake. As we were approaching South Rona I went forward to take the jib down and asked my wife to keep well up to windward as the flood setting south-east through the Sound was strong. The jib down I went below to get the C.Q.R. ready and again repeated my request, in fact I did so several times and my wife, obedient on this occasion, did as I asked. When I came up on deck again I could not make out where we had got to. We scraped past some rocks on starboard which should not have been there, and then some on port. To add to our worry the wind increased, but by topping the boom, when not watching for rocks, I managed to slow her up a bit. I was on the point of turning back, or trying to do so, when most fortunately I saw a fishing boat coming out by the correct passage and

SCALPAY SOUND. See photograph, page 96.

saw at once the mistake we had made. We had come to wind-ward of Rough Island, which is so like the rough hummocks of Rona itself that we had not identified it. We ought to have noticed sooner that instead of an island to the north-west of us there was nothing but a collection of rocks, some awash, and that we had not seen the house at the head of the bay which shows the channel.

As I had the large scale chart No. 2570 (Northern part of Sound of Raasay and Inner Sound) on deck once our mistake was appreciated we were able to find our way in without touching anything.

When later in the day I was telling Christopher Macrae of how cleverly I had retrieved my mistake, he rather squashed me by saying " the big steamers often come in that way." He was, as I expected, very critical of our new boat, especially of her high mast. I told him that I had taken 3 ft. 6 in. off it, but he replied, " well, you should take off another six feet." The two brothers had not changed at all, but the sister seemed to be more troubled than ever with rheumatism.

The weather now threatened to break down as we had strong winds again, and next day it rained heavily and steadily. This did not prevent my wife tramping all over the island in oilskins and gum boots accompanied by " Jack." She found it strange to be wandering over an island that was once in-habited and is now almost deserted, as so many of our northern islands are. At one time there had been a " big township " in Acarsaid Tioram (the " harbour which dries out.") Where there had been men and women busy working and children playing there are now only ruined cottages, an empty school and a desolate church with its old-fashioned pulpit and rude wooden benches. The " Widow's Cot " in the Big Harbour, still shown in Chart 2570, no longer exists unless the stone shed near the shore was part of it. The story is that after the owner had been drowned when missing the entrance on a dirty night, his widow kept a lamp burning every night to guide others into shelter. The Macraes house, called " The Lodge," is a little bit up from the shore and has few comforts or conveniences. This is the house that is, or should be, the guide to the channel.

At the south end of the island there had been another village, but the small houses are now in ruins. Close to it is a deserted graveyard with a small stone building also in ruins. This looks across the Sound of Raasay where the people now reside, who once lived in this lonely island and whose forebears now rest in their graves here.

I had a visit from the Raasay-Rona postman who reminded me that I had operated on him some fourteen years before in Glasgow. He seems quite fit for his arduous job, which includes walking over many miles of rough paths and rowing across Rona Sound twice a week in all weathers ; so I seem to have done him no harm. We had dinner with (the late) Tom Guthrie who had come in in *Elspeth*, and who acted as our postman next day by taking a batch of letters for us to Portree.

And then we set off to make our third mistake. Sailing out, taking the correct channel this time, we found a heavy swell outside and with the dinghy doing its best to hit us we ran past Eil. Tigh into the inlet between *Eil. Fladda* and Raasay. I asked my wife to carry on until she saw the school-house which is marked on Chart 2570 and then to round up, while I went below for the anchor. When I came up again I noticed, only just in time, that we were on the point of charg-ing the bar which separates the north and south anchorages. My wife had again been all too obedient. She had not seen the schoolhouse, nor indeed any houses, because standing some distance back from the edge of the cliff they are invisible from the water. It was entirely my fault this time as I ought to have noticed the double shore line on the chart and appreci-ated that this indicated a cliff. It was nearly high water when we came in, and we saw what a " let off " we had had when the falling tide exposed a really horrible causeway of big boulders which are used as stepping-stones at low water.

As we anchored a row of eight little heads appeared at the edge of the cliff just above us. Going ashore in the evening we found a very happy family in one of the cottages, and had with us just sufficient chocolate to go round. They had come originally from South Rona where the grandfather had been the missionary. This is a most unusual place, a gut with high cliffs on both sides, and we were glad when the northerly took off before we turned in as, while it may be safe, it might be very uncomfortable.

Hoping that our series of stupid mistakes was now at an end we crossed the Inner Sound to Loch Torridon anchoring, as in 1933, at *Kenmore* in *Loch Creagach*, and without any more delay the bad weather not only came but stayed. I had previously made a note in the log that in giving us so many warnings the meteorological experts are taking extra good care of us this summer, but for the next six days we had not merely the warnings but the gales themselves.

There is, perhaps, too much about the weather in this narrative, but this is a subject of predominant interest on the west coast of Scotland especially when one is living in a small yacht. For the next week it was so indescribably bad that my remarks about it will be as discreet and brief as possible.

The swell we had noticed outside showed that the morning forecast of " winds increasing in the north " had been correct, and although we had anchored as far in as we dared on the north side of the bay we could still feel it. No sooner were we in than a warning arrived and with it a north-westerly gale and heavy rain. We were chagrined next day to hear that England and the southern half of Scotland were to enjoy " light variable winds due to an anticyclone off the west of Ireland," while we were to endure a " westerly gale due to a deep depression off Iceland." That unfair state of affairs continued for five more days, the only change being that as the depression enveloped us the wind backed to the south-west and south, and we lost some of our shelter. How we tossed about ! We heeled over in the squalls, we rolled, we pitched, our counter slammed and thumped so loudly that it was difficult to believe that the dinghy was not under it, and the shrieking of the wind in the shrouds kept my wife awake.

An angel slipped a few fathoms down the chain steadied us a little, and with our heavier C.Q.R. and twenty-five fathoms of chain I felt confident that we would stay put so long as nothing carried away. After five nights of this violent motion we deserted ship and had a good sleep on a very hard mattress in the tiny attic of one of the cottages, but we felt a little ashamed of this and were glad to get back on board. We had thought of shifting over to Loch Beg, a small inlet completely sheltered from the south, but had decided against this as if the wind shifted to the north we would have been caught in a nasty trap. We consoled ourselves by hoping that we were using up all the bad weather before Charlie came north to join us, but we

KENMORE. See Frontispiece and painting, page 113.

were beginning to wonder where and how he would find us

The " village " here consists of five small cottages and the inhabitants, who have very little English, are almost isolated from the outside world. There is no road, merely a " bridle path " seven miles to Shieldaig or fourteen miles round the coast to Applecross. We were told that when a Department or Board had been asked for a road they had been given a telephone at Arrina-crinnach as it was cheaper !

We managed to get ashore every day—we had to for " Jack's " benefit ; we walked to Arrina-crinnach (" The Shieling of the Wheat ") to 'phone and to talk with the sister and brother there ; we walked half-way to Shieldaig and had a fine view of the 3,000 ft. high Ben Alligin and Liathach towering behind Loch Torridon ; we walked to Fearn Mor and seeing what it was like outside, were thankful for the comparative shelter we had in our bay ; my wife sketched a lot ; we were sorry to see how far it was from the cottages to the peat beds, but I am afraid we did not offer to help ; we watched a Harris woman weaving; and taking advantage of the antics of the boat I washed out the bilges very thoroughly. And so the time passed.

Fortunately we had stocked up the larder at Portree and we were able to get fresh milk every day, but we ran short of meat. I asked about this ashore and was told that someone was coming some day to kill somebody's sheep. When we were turning in the following evening at 10 p.m. I heard a man hailing us and found a big lugsail alongside with the " butcher " and the remnants of the sheep. The wind had taken off temporarily, but in the jabble of sea it was really queer to see him trying to weigh a couple of pounds with a spring balance—a unique shopping transaction. With a cheery " good-night " he set off for his home at Fearn Mor some three miles down the loch side.

My wife did a dreadful thing one day. For use with the primus stoves I had a tin which I kept filled with methylated spirits from a quart bottle. She spoke of some difficulty in getting this to light and I discovered that she had filled the tin from the whisky bottle, and it was my last one and now nearly empty. Perhaps she has done this before, and perhaps, just perhaps, this explains why these bottles seem to empty so quickly at sea. But she was forgiven when, most dexterously, she cut my hair that afternoon.

VII

Southward Bound Again

ON the sixth day the gale took off and after another day we got away but not without a struggle. The faithful C.Q.R. had bitten so deeply into the sea bed that it brought up an enormous mass of seaweed and it was a good twenty minutes before I got rid of it. Until it was more or less cleared we were not under control, but fortunately the wind was light. (Had we decided to shift during the gale we might have had great difficulty in keeping off the lee shore.)

A fishing skiff had come in the day before and as we were passing Arrina-crinnach she came out with the body of an old man and a large funeral party on board. Because of the absence of a road they were taking this unusual way of getting to the burial ground at Applecross. (We heard later that they had been unable to land there and had gone on to Poll Creadha.)

For several hours we made slow progress in fairly thick mist down the Inner Sound as the southerly was light and fickle. Remembering the morning forecast of " winds freshening from the west," I kept over to the Rona shore so that if necessary we could lie Poll Doin. When nearing the south end of Rona I noticed a big black cloud driving off the Cuillins and wondered if it was coming our way, but it passed on to the east. Having been told that a cloud driven off the Cuillins should be treated as a forerunner of very heavy squalls, I changed from light to storm jib, although we had had so little wind that I had switched on the engine. Another cloud then came driving up over Dun Caan, Raasay and we were suddenly struck by a very severe squall and I set about pulling down a couple of reefs. Having topped the boom I had no difficulty with the luff tackle, but I had a troublesome time on the counter as we could not keep the boat head to wind. The batten was loath to come out and, being perhaps a trifle rough with the reef earing, I pulled the cringle out and the sail tore for about one foot. The leech-rope was all that was holding it, but by topping the boom more (I had two lifts) and nursing the sail in the squalls we managed to make the narrow passage between

Eil. Fraoich and Eil. Sheamairach without the tear spreading. Thankful that the sail had not ripped right across we ran into *Acarsaid Mor*.

I should really have dropped the sail and got the trysail up, but I was unwilling to fall back to leeward as we were rather close to the Rona shore. Had I anticipated so much trouble I would of course have taken off the jib, but I thought the engine would hold her up. The real cause of the mishap was the fact that the cringle had been merely stamped through the sail instead of being worked into the leech-rope. This was more a misadventure than a mistake, so I will not add it to the other three.

We spent a couple of hours mending the tear and making a new cringle, roped this time, before going ashore. We then heard that " all the skiffs " had sheltered here during the gale and that one of them had taken seventeen hours from the Shiant Islands. This, however, is difficult to believe. The *Cutty Sark* had been in and there was a rumour that " a wee red yacht was missing." I hope nobody is looking for us. We are worried about " Jack " ; he was in good form yesterday, but to-day is listless and can hardly stand. He seems to have been poisoned.

By evening it was blowing gale force and as there were three skiffs behind the island we were lying in the channel, and were not too comfortable. When my wife baked scones for the crew of the *Isa Wood* they replied with herring. I was in their fo'c'sle when they were having a meal. Although they used neither knives, forks nor spoons, the bare table was spotlessly clean and they all washed their hands after the meal in a bucket of salt water. They had very, very little comfort, but there were no grumbles.

" Jack " was worse next day and my wife was very anxious to get him to a vet.; we had also to meet Charlie and could not get in touch with him from here. So when I heard that the *Isa Wood* was leaving in the evening to look for herring, asked if they would tow us to *Portree*. They consented, but said it would be very wet. It certainly was, as they took us at seven knots and we were soaked before we got to Portree. I went ashore and tried, but without success, to 'phone Charlie. But I was lucky to find the vet. and after he had seen " Jack " on board he took him ashore.

It was midnight before we were ready to turn in after a rather worrying day. Just as I was getting into my bed, one of *Cutty Sark's* crew came alongside ; it was very dark and raining heavily and as he had an enormous sou'wester on I could not make out who he was at first. They had seen us running into Acarsaid Mor when they were lifting their pots at Eil. Tigh and had come to give us some lobsters. These people certainly believe in the comradeship of the sea even when they meet amateurs like ourselves. They were leaving early to return to Kyle Akin so I gave him a note to leave at the Post Office there for Charlie. He put it on the top of his head under his sou'wester !

Charlie arriving at Kyle Akin made enquiries at the Post Office as arranged, and getting my note came on to Portree by bus. We had to-day the explanation of the rumour that we were missing. My wife 'phoning to Kyle Akin in the morning was told that a Mr. R. had been hunting for me for the last fortnight, 'phoning and wiring from all sorts of places. He was now at Gairloch, so I wired him to come to Portree if he wanted to see me. He arrived at 11 p.m. having had no end of trouble getting his Baby Austin across various ferries after closing time.

He had been told by someone that I was probably at Kyle Akin so had set off in his car from Glasgow, and missing us at Kyle had tried Portree, Plockton, Shieldaig and Gairloch. The reason for this importunity was that, being examined and found fit by the medical officers of the Air Ministry, he was told that before he could be accepted for an appointment he must get a certificate from me as I had operated on him some eighteen years before. He was determined to find me as he intended getting married if he got the appointment.

Luckily I remembered about the operation and after a perfunctory examination in the cabin, my wife and Charlie being banished to the cockpit, I gave him the certificate he had certainly earned. As his hunt had been more prolonged than he had anticipated he had run short of cash and had been spending most of his nights trying to sleep in his car. (I heard later that he had been accepted by both the Air Ministry and his fiancée. If, as I hope, he has since then played an important part in the work of the Ministry that somewhat weird medical examination at midnight in a six-metre in Portree Bay may have helped the " War Effort.")

Sonas came in next day reefed, but when the northerly wind took off in the afternoon we left for the south. (" Jack " whom we left in the vet.'s care, was already moribund and died next day.) We passed *Kentra* beating up the Sound, and although quite a long way off she recognized us and dipped ; a courteous greeting from a big sister. We ran through a big school of basking sharks at the Point of Ayre, and then with a failing wind had a slow drift through the Kyle to *Loch na Beist*, where we anchored beside *The Ketch*. Dinner at 10.30 p.m. and to bed at midnight.

Dr. Riddell wakened us next morning as they were leaving, and when we were at breakfast N.L. turned up. He was finding life rather dull alone on *Mingaly* at Kyle of Loch Alsh, so we sent away the gig in which he had come and gave him a lively sail to *Totaig*. After lunch, leaving Charlie busy mending a primus stove, we rowed N.L. across to Dornie and saw him off on foot for Kyle. On our return Charlie was still working at the stove ! Later he created a record for this ship by catching seven fish when rowing back from Leiter Fearn. A gale we had been told about in the morning did not arrive, but by evening the rain descended " in buckets."

We left Totaig next morning, under power, after a huge breakfast of fish, but at the red buoy the engine stopped. Charlie tried " this and that " without success and then we discovered that the propeller had got completely matted up with seaweed. Getting through Kyle Rhea with the very last of the ebb we had a slow beat to—yes, to *Mallaig*. The southerly had brought dense mist and it was not wise to continue, but why did we not go into Loch Nevis ? (see p. 52).

We paid for our mistake, as by 4 a.m. it was blowing straight into the harbour from the north, and we were almost foul of a motor boat riding to a very short mooring. I looked out once or twice and was then told by my wife, " For goodness sake stop getting up and down," so, taking in five of our twenty fathoms of chain I retired to my bed again. We had to shift an hour later, but as visibility was absolutely nil, we did not leave the bay uncomfortable as it was.

The mist cleared a little after lunch and we had a fast and somewhat wet reach across to *Eigg*. We were wet below as well, as Charlie upset the milk-can for the second time since Portree. We were then held up at Eigg for three days by fresh southerly winds, and it was not too comfortable as the tide held us across the wind and a considerable swell came in from the south. We rolled a lot and we pitched a lot, and in the clear intervals we looked at Ardnamurchan Lighthouse and wondered how soon we would be past it.

We explored the cave in which the MacDonalds had been suffocated by the MacLeods. The entrance is so small and so well concealed that those hiding in it would not have been discovered had not one of them gone out to see if the MacLeods had left. He was seen by them as they were on the point of leaving and his footmarks in the snow led them to the cave. My wife and I walked across the island but did not reach the Singing Sands, and Charlie climbed the Scuir in dense mist, but we finally got away one morning very early with no wind and " a simply beastly swell." With the lighthouse abeam we picked up a breeze and ran into *Tobormory* where to our surprise we found that the moorings of The Western Isles Yacht Club were at last laid, on July 10th !

We got a fine batch of letters and papers which we enjoyed reading when beating down the Sound next day to *Puillodo-bhrain*. There was much talk that evening of visiting the Garvellochs, but next morning's forecast of " winds veering to the south and becoming strong," was not encouraging, so we gave up the idea and sailed to *Craobh, Loch Shuna*. There we lay for three days with strong winds and incessant driving rain. We walked to Gemmil Farm for eggs ; we rowed to Arduaine to 'phone and we took the bus from Lunga Gate to Oban for stores and baths.

On the third day as the rain had stopped we beat down the Sound of Jura to the *Small Isles* where we enjoyed a beautiful afternoon and evening with friends ashore. To our surprise the fine weather continued, and we had a pleasant sail next day to *Charsaig, Cantyre*, where lying behind the island we found the kind of anchorage we fancy. There is good shelter and yet no feeling of being shut in as the open Sound is so near. Summer seemed to have come at last as next day was again fine and very warm when, leaving by the north channel, we sailed round to *Crinan Harbour*. As I was not feeling well we moved later into the Basin where, in the evening the yachts taking part in the C.C. Club's race from Rothesay to Tobormory arrived.

It was very hot next day, but big black clouds were gathering so perhaps we were wrong about the advent of summer. As neither my wife nor I was feeling too brisk we stayed there another night and then went through the canal to *Ardrishaig*. Charlie was due back at work so he left by steamer, and as soon as he had gone the rain descended in cascades.

The following day we had a fast sail to the Kyles of Bute, anchoring at *Wood Farm Buoy* just before the Heavens again opened and down came the rain. There was a terrible lot of chain-grinding during the night as we were not far enough in to be out of the tide, and we must have been lying stern to the wind as the cabin floor was awash in the morning. The chain had wrapped itself round a rock and it was only after a lot of manœuvring under sail that we got it free when lifting anchor.

Being so near home we ignored a gale warning, our fifteenth this cruise, and set off for Rhu. We had a fast run to Toward Point, but after gybing there we found more wind than we wanted off the Cowal shore with a big sea running up the Firth. The dinghy was having a bad time and we really ought to have reefed, but as we were just managing to lie our course without gybing again we carried on. When near Roseneath Patch, where there was a lot of broken water, the dinghy painter carried away. We soon made contact with it, rather too violent contact I confess, and shackled on the spare painter, but shortly afterwards the dinghy which was half full, took a dive and filled completely. It was a tricky job, and a very wet one too, getting it alongside and baling it out with the bucket, as neither the sea nor the wind had gone down. So with this rather strenuous incident at the end of a seven-knot run from Colintraive we finished our two months' cruise and picked up our moorings at Rhu on July 21st.

We had had extraordinarily bad weather ; out of fifty-eight days there had been continuous rain on fourteen, and on only eighteen was there much sunshine. Our experience with various strengths of wind was also unusual ; light to moderate on thirty-two ; fresh to strong on sixteen and gales on ten of the fifteen days on which we had warnings. " Jack's " illness and death had distressed us and we had been unlucky in meeting so few of our sailing friends, but in spite of this we had enjoyed a fine cruise.

* * *

Two days before setting off on our cruise I had taken part in the opening race of the season at Hunter's Quay with Charlie and R.S. as my crew. With all our cruising gear and stores on board and with our reduced sail area we were soon left behind in the light south-easterly by *Blink*, a Swedish ex-six-metre. Fortunately the wind strengthened considerably and passing her on a windward leg we drew ahead and won by three minutes. The third boat was far behind.

A few days after our return we joined the fleet racing from Hunter's Quay to Tarbert, Loch Fyne, my wife, Bob and Neill being with me. As the ebb was strong and there was no wind, several boats fouled the mark at the start and many were across too soon, but using our anchor we kept out of trouble. It was a very slow beat to Toward and through the Kyles and we did not round Ardlamont till 9 p.m. well up with our section. Drifting across to the Cantyre shore, hoping to get the benefit of the flood there, we ghosted along in pitch darkness with the lightest of airs towards Tarbert. It was quite eerie as only when some boat showed a light or a crew amused themselves with a fog-horn or even spoke did we have any evidence that we were not absolutely alone. At 1 a.m. in the beam of the Commodore's searchlight we spotted *Blink*, whom we had last seen at Ardlamont, coming in on starboard tack. We were on port but were able to make the line ahead of her and got a first in our class.

Leaving out the six starts in the Clyde Fortnight in 1935 when we were so " foul and slow," we had in these three years got seven firsts and four seconds in eleven starts. Racing had been a secondary consideration with us, but we had had a great deal of pleasurable excitement out of it. The family too had been infected by the racing fever. Charlie was now part owner of a *Dragon* and Bob had won the Cup in the University and School races in the Gareloch two years in succession. (John and Neill were to be keen competitors later.)

* * *

When lying at Kenmore, Loch Torridon, I had made up my mind that it was not fair to expect my wife to come cruising for any length of time without more comfort and convenience. What we missed were a good cooking stove, a plentiful supply of water, room for stores and clothes, a w.c. and more protection when sailing.

We had enjoyed our three years with this boat so much, both when cruising and racing, that it was hard indeed to think of losing her, and when we at last decided to sell her we were fortunate in getting a buyer who would make full use and be as proud of her as we had been.

So *Rowan III* was sold and McGruers were asked to build a boat which my wife and I could handle easily, with a small sail area, an engine of sufficient power to drive us against a strong head wind and sea, and in which we could cruise for long periods with all the comfort and conveniences which we feel we have earned at our somewhat advanced age.

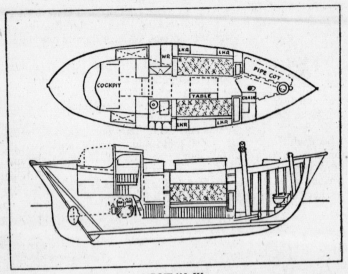

ROWAN IV.

L.O.A. 29ft. 6ins. L.W.L. 26ft. Beam 9ft. Draft 4ft. 9ins. Tonnage T.M. 8.8 tons.

PART IV

The Leaves are Turning—1938 to 1939

I

Rowan IV. A Loch Fyne Type

ROWAN IV's hull was at my request modelled on the Loch Fyne fishing skiff, but she had a gaff mainsail and jib instead of the usual lugsail. Her principal measurements were :—*length overall* 29 ft. 6 in.; *length waterline* 26 ft.; *beam* 9 ft.; *draft* 4 ft. 9 in.; *tonnage T.M.* 8.8 tons; *sail area* 342 sq. ft. Her iron keel weighed 2¼ tons and there were a few pigs of lead ballast inside. She had two bilge keels, 10 ft. by 5 in.

Her *sails* were tanned ; the main, 247 sq. ft. had two reefs ; the jibs 95 and 50 sq. ft. hanked to the forestay ; there were no runners, the shrouds being placed far aft ; there was a *mast-winch* with a drum which was useful for the throat halyards and a gipsy for the anchor chain.

The addition of a short *bowsprit* requires some explanation. It was to obviate the necessity of lifting the 45-lb. C.Q.R., perhaps heavily loaded with seaweed, on board when getting under weigh. In addition to the usual double roller stem-head gammon iron it had a bowsprit crance over which the chain was passed. When the mast-winch was operated, without any back-breaking exertion, the shank of the anchor fell automatically along the bowsprit and could be quickly secured to it by a lanyard until it was convenient to bring it on board.

The *cockpit* was large with a small *deck-shelter* at its forward end. This had armour-plate glass windows at the sides and forward. A continuous steel channel bar from one bilge stringer to the other across the top of it carried the mainsheet horse. In this " dog-house " were two comfortably broad seats.

Forward of this was a trunk which gave plenty of space above the galley on starboard, 6 ft. headroom amidships, and on port a *meat safe* which was ventilated from outside but was accessible from inside by means of sliding doors. It would have been an advantage below if this trunk had been carried as far forward as the skylight, but this was sacrificed so as to allow an 8-ft. *dinghy* to be carried on deck. This, with the middle thwart removed, fitted snugly over the sky-light between the trunk and the mast.

The deck was covered with canvas and the 2-in. teak rail had very large scuppers. (Why are these usually far too small ?) A canvas cockpit cover supported on removable stanchions was for use at anchor in wet weather, or when the family invaded the ship and extra berths were required. There was a lot of space for stowing gear under the short counter and large lockers at the sides of the cockpit for bos'n's stores, spare Calor gas locker container, etc.

On the starboard side of the companion was the *galley* with a Calor gas stove, a drip-board and basin, a bulkhead type pump, racks for crockery and lockers for pots and pans. On port below the meat safe was a large store cupboard and forward of it a wardrobe. The bulkhead between this and the cabin was cut away in the form of a flattened letter omega, with curtain but no door. This, with the skylight, gave us a well-lit, easily ventilated cabin.

As the *cabin* was 8 ft. long it contained all we needed for comfort both at night and during the day. The settees were upholstered with 6 ft. by 2 ft. by 4 in. Dunlopillo cushions and the backs, which were portable, by 6 ft. by 18 ins. by 3 in. ones. Behind these the sides of the ship were lined by narrow battens. Above the settees were broad shelves with lockers and room for a Schooner wireless set and a small barograph; at the aft end convenient to both cabin and galley were lockers for glasses, bottles, etc. Forward on starboard was a large locker recessed into the fo'c'sle for stores and all sorts of odds and ends, and on port a bookcase and chart locker. The flap of the table, which was fixed to the floor, was removable and formed the door to the companion when at moorings.

Below the settees were two 25-gall. *water tanks* with a communicating pipe on which there was an accessible cock. Water was drawn from here by the pump in the galley, but I fitted up in addition a small 2-gall. tank at the forward end of the cockpit for fresh drinking water.

In the *fo'c'sle* there was on port a pipe cot (for occasional use), an " S.L." w.c. in the forepeak, a spare 45-lb. Fisherman and a basin on starboard, and on the bulkhead a 30-fathom $2\frac{1}{4}$ in. warp. The *chain locker* was fitted directly below the gipsy of the mast-winch on the starboard side of the mast; it had a vertical division and the 35 fathoms of $\frac{3}{8}$-in. chain was self-stowing. There was a grating at the foot of the locker with a flap-door for cleaning it out.

A 15 h.p. 4-cyl. *Kelvin Engine* was installed under the cockpit floor where it was readily accessible. It had reverse gear, solid propeller, water-jacketed silencer, dynamo and self-starter—what more could one ask for? Two 15-gall. petrol tanks were housed under the deck at the side of the cockpit with interrupted filling pipes and accessible turn-off cocks. A low bulkhead prevented any leakage forward from the engine bilges, for which there was a semi-rotary pump. A Vortex centrifugal *pump* just forward of this could, if required keep the rest of the ship dry. We had *electric light* throughout with miniature fittings and an inspection plug near the engine.

II

1938 : Fair Weather and Foul

ROWAN IV was launched with due ceremony, Mary feeling very important as she broke a bottle of the best on the stem. For two weeks I was so busy finishing odds and ends, taking out stores and gear and filling up the water tanks that we did not have time to leave moorings for even a short trial cruise.

* * *

Cruise to Muck and Round Mull : May 24th to June 30th.— My wife, " Righ " and myself ; later Mary and a friend, M.R.

Full of confidence that all our arrangements would prove satisfactory we hoisted sail for the first time and left Rhu on May 24th hoping not only to re-visit our old haunts but to find some new ones before returning at the end of June.

In fair weather with a moderate westerly and finally with the help of the engine we reached Ardrishaig after a night at *Colintraive.* " Righ," our springer spaniel, was with us and as he was as agile on board as ashore and in very good form we thought that he was going to be the perfect sailor.

The good weather did not last long ; before we got to *Crinan* it was raining and our cockpit cover was tested, and not found wanting, by a downpour during the night. *Nova* was in the Basin and we had a long visit from T. N. Arkle. He is a charming but most independent man, refusing to have a meal with us although his cooking facilities were very meagre.

Passing through the Dorus Mor next day the flood was kicking up so much sea against the fresh westerly that we were literally tossed all over the place and took a lot of water on deck. The skylight had inadvertently been left partly open under the dinghy and a good deal found its way into the cabin. This and the violent motion scared " Righ " and was the beginning of future trouble. A fast run up Shuna Sound took us to *Ardinamir* where it poured and poured all evening and all night.

Lifting anchor for the first time next morning and finding that with the mast-winch it was child's play, we sailed out of the bay and then in Cuan Sound very nearly came to grief. My wife at the tiller, mistaking Sgeir Bodach for the Cleit Rock, was serenely heading for a horrible collection of rocks when I fortunately looked out from the forehatch just in time.

With the help of the flood and a light south-westerly we were soon in the Sound of Mull, but being headed at the Green Island motored to *Tobormory* entering by the Doirlinn Narrows one hour before high water. For two hours on each side of high water there is at least six feet, or when the base of the perch is covered there is eight feet of water, so with a leading wind or under power this short-cut presents no difficulties.

And now we were to find out that we had been over-confident and that our arrangements were not all perfect. There was some swell coming into the Bay and even though our motion was not at all violent there was in what should have been the silence of the night a most disconcerting splashing in the water tanks so close under our berths. We got little or no sleep and how I cursed the makers of these tanks for having, as I soon discovered, omitted to put in any baffle plates. I pumped out most of the water I had so laboriously taken on board at Rhu and hoped that with the tanks only a quarter full there would be no more splashing. This proved to be correct, but of course we had not full use of them until after our return home the omission was put right.

As it was cold, wet and windy we sailed across to *The Gut, Oronsay*, and were delighted when the weather cleared and the evening was warm and sunny. We had recommended this anchorage to two Nottingham couples in a motor boat at Tobormory and they came in later and were charmed with the place and the weather. But down went the glass and with a poor forecast there was one of our old bugbears, a gale warning. Surely we are not going to have last summer's weather over again. (We were !)

Next morning we got away purposely before the forecast, but it found us off Ardnamurchan plugging under engine against a fresh north-westerly and repeated its warning. We had often intended visiting *Muck*, so we thought this was a good opportunity and so did poor " Righ," who was very upset by the motion. Even the small barograph was protesting as could be seen from the smudges of the recording pen. This instrument was very accurate, but I had already noticed after our tossing in the Dorus Mor that, like the dog, it objected to rough water.

With the help of a chart which Mr. MacEwan had given me some years before, we found our way into Port Mor anchoring well up the bay in three fathoms. The lines " west end of Eigg open east of Muck " and " Road on crest of hill in line with south chimney of house at end of pier " make it easy to clear Bogha Ruadh and the one-fathom rock north of Dubh Sgeir.

After lunch we walked across the island, which is low, flat and green, to Gallanach Bay where the swell which was already coming in would have made that anchorage very uncomfortable. The view was perfect ; the white sand, the blue water, Eigg and Rum not far away and the mountains of Skye in the distance ; but we thought how much more sheltered we were at Port Mor. We had tea with the MacEwans in their charming house, and Mr. MacEwan walking back with us along a cliff path came on board to see our ship.

By this time it was blowing hard from the north-west, and although we had shelter from that quarter we were rolling, rolling, rolling as we lay across the swell that was coming round the corner at high water. We tried in vain to stop the rattle and noise with all the socks, stockings, jerseys, towels and newspapers on board. So I hurriedly rowed up to the jetty at the head of the bay and finding that there was one fathom all the way, decided that that was the place for us. We lifted anchor and motored in and, assisted by the islanders, tied up on the north side of the jetty just in time, half an hour after high water. This was a new experience for us, which I had been loath to suggest, but when I asked my wife if she would object if we lay up against a pier, she replied, " I'd lie up against anything to get away from all this noise."

When we turned in, the boat sitting comfortably on a smooth sandy bottom with a list to the jetty and the throat halyards round a huge stone, it was blowing gale force outside, and we knew we had done the right thing. This was confirmed in the morning when the wind had backed and was blowing straight into the bay.

The islanders with Highland courtesy were nowhere to be seen when we had anchored, but were only too willing to help when we came in later. They were surprised that we knew of their harbour and of the way in. I was glad to be able to repay to some extent their kindness by arranging for the admission to my old hospital in Glasgow of an old man who had a dangerous ulcer on his face. Some persuasion was necessary as he thought he was too old to be cured of anything, but he made a perfect recovery.

The tides were taking off, and as we did not wish to be " grounded " here for a fortnight we left two days later in spite of unsettled weather and the usual warning. The wind was north-west so we sailed south-west, and off Caliach Point ran into a very confused sea but found it much less disturbing under sail than when motoring.

Looking for the entrance to *Acarsaid Mor, Gometra,* I stupidly got into the bay to the east of it where there are a number of rocks well off-shore, but fortunately got clear and anchored in the harbour just inside the entrance in one and a quarter fathoms. We had a walk ashore and saw a wonderful sunset over the Treshnish Isles. To offset this we had yet another warning. " This evening announcement is becoming monotonous." The reef of rocks at the narrow entrance did not prevent a considerable swell from coming in, and as there was not enough water for us any further up the bay, we had just to roll and bear it.

We had difficulty in getting ashore in the morning, but found a delightfully warm sheltered spot on Eil. Dioghulum. As the evening news told of a hurricane in the south of England we must not complain about our mere gale, which, thank goodness, seems now to be moderating.

After two rather restless days we were not sorry to leave and sailed round to *Ulva Sound.* The note in the C.C.C. Journal about this channel between Ulva and Mull is over-cautious. It states that it is " winding and intricate and studded with rocks and islets " and that " it is advisable to use the lead constantly." But using Chart 3015 (Loch na Keal) there should be no difficulty. We identified the three-feet high rock north of Torr Ardalum and then found our way down one hour before high water, anchoring at the south end of Eil. a Chaolais in three fathoms. We were impressed with the peacefulness here and spent the day writing letters, walking to the Post Office, where we got three recent papers, 'phoning Charlie and getting milk at the Ferry Inn. We were told

ULVA SOUND. See painting, page 147.

that the best anchorage was in the bay inside Anchor Point, but in our ignorance we saw no reason for shifting. Little did we dream of the strange weather we were to have, nor did we think it would be ten days before we moved on.

Getting a forecast next morning of southerly winds we took the advice which had been given and moved down to Anchor Point, dropping the C.Q.R. in one and three quarter fathoms, but hardly far enough in as we were to find out later. In bright sunshine we rowed across to the east jetty and walked to Oskamull Farm. By the time we got back to the dinghy it was blowing so hard that only with difficulty did I manage to row across to the other jetty. My wife and " Righ " then walked along the shore and I rejoined them to windward of the yacht after a hard struggle, and so we got on board. By evening we were riding to twenty fathoms chain with an angel down. This sudden violent change was typical of what we were to have for the next ten days.

A day of continuous sunshine was then followed by two days of continuous rain and a southerly gale. At midnight as the wind was from the south-east, and Sgeir Beul a Chaolais being covered was giving us little or no protection, I was really worried. Spindrift was flying all over the place, we were heeling over in the squalls and Sgeir Lach was uncomfortably close under our lee. The glass fell two-tenths in two hours and then rose the same amount, but to our relief the wind veered to south-west at 4 a.m. and we now had shelter from the Point.

There is only one spot here, but it is a good one, where one can get shelter from the squalls from Ben More. It is between Sgeir Beul and Sgeir Lach a little south of the line closing Anchor Point and Eil. Casach, just at the three-quarter fathom mark on Charts 3015 and 2652 (Loch Tuadh and the Isles.) There are one and a quarter fathoms here at low water.

After four days here we thought we would explore the north anchorage, so at half-flood motored round Anvil Point and anchored beside a four-ton Watson-designed yawl in the bay below the church. There was shelter here from the south which appealed to us, but precious little water, and we had to be content with one fathom at low water. We had come through this channel twice and only now discovered an uncharted rock, awash at low water. It is at the letter " m " on Charts 3015 and 2652, about halfway between the " A " of Anvil Point and the " dries three-feet " reef on the north side.

The vagaries of the weather followed us here ; strong winds, heavy showers, with intervals of light airs and warm sunshine. On one day of continuous sunshine my wife did a big washing ashore and I got all our clothes and bedding aired. We walked a lot, here and there, which " Righ " thoroughly enjoyed, and we spent quite a lot of time trying to meet the butcher's and grocer's carts whose comings and goings were very irregular. My wife, interested as ever in things of the past, wanted to find the house in which Dr. Johnson had spent a night. Knocking at the door of the cottage to which she had been directed and asking about it she was told that they " did not know any one of that name here." The two brothers who run the ferry came on board one day after pumping out the yawl, and later we had a visit from her owner, an Edinburgh man who spends his week-ends here. He said that the peacefulness of the place more than made up for the long tiring journey by train, steamer, post van and ferry.

And then Mary and her friend, M.R., arrived, and some of the peace was lost. They brought with them a large cake, a huge bunch of bananas, a " stationery stall of periodicals," nine large flagons of cider and much laughter and good humour. By packing all this and the three ladies and " Righ " into the eight-foot dinghy and rowing them to the yacht against the ebb, I performed a miracle. Mary and her friend slept ashore, and rather upset the routine of the ship by coming on board still full of sleep at about 11 a.m. and demanding breakfast.

After ten days of real Scotch mixture of weather we left, but the purveyor of warnings had not done with us, for almost before we had passed Inch Kenneth he gave us another. There was some mist in Loch na Keal and I was glad when we were safely past Macquarrie Rock. It then cleared and we had an exhilarating sail in bright sunshine to Loch Lathaich, but M.R. did not enjoy it and " Righ " sympathised with her. There was some collusion between my wife, who thinks that I " never go in far enough," and Mary who was in charge of the lead, but I spotted their little game in time, and the anchor went down in one and a half fathoms at the mouth of *Loch Caol, Loch Lathaich*. As most of the loch to their surprise dried out later I think she was satisfied this time.

THE LEAVES ARE TURNING—1938-1939

Next day I rowed the three ladies to the head of the loch, where we got a most courteous welcome from the proprietor, and they got a car to Fionnphort and spent the day on Iona. When having lunch there they got into conversation with a Mr. P. who with a clerical friend had sailed from Oban in an open home-built boat with two small sails and heavily-laden with all sort of gear. Like Lewis Carroll's *White Knight* they wished to be " provided for everything," so included in their cargo a tent, mountaineering boots, pots and pans, but no mouse traps, beehives or fire-irons.

In their absence I enjoyed a quiet afternoon polishing the mahogany of the cabin and having a snooze. (That deserves a paragraph all to itself !)

It had been blowing hard all day from the north-west and during the night we lay across the swell which seemed to be looking specially for us ; and how we rolled. It reminded me of Kipling's words, " That storm blew by but left behind her anchor-shiftin' swell," and although we had no fear of our anchor moving we got no sleep after 5 a.m.

I managed to get the shore party on board by 10 a.m., a record, and leaving under power we punched our way against a fresh northerly until we opened the Sound of Iona. Hoisting sail and switching off the engine we then had a fine run down the Sound, inside the Torranan Rocks and along the south of Mull as far as the Firth of Lorn before we lost the wind at Eil. Straideun, averaging more than five knots. I was surprised and disappointed that neither Mary nor her friend seemed to appreciate the joy of surging along in a small craft with the high cliffs of Mull to port and the open sea to starboard, the sun high overhead in a blue sky and the blue water flecked with white waves.

We then motored up the Mull shore into *Loch Spelve* where we anchored beside *Hyskeir* in the north-west corner. After a delightfully quiet night we ran out of the loch and got as far as Duart Point before we had to call on the Kelvin to take us to Tobormory for stores and letters. In the evening we sailed across to *Drumbuy*, where to our surprise we had another quiet night followed by a lovely sunny morning. Why, we said, did we not get this fine weather a fortnight ago ?

Returning to *Tobermory* we found *White Cloud* and *Nova* there and we saw quite a lot of T. N. Arkle. He kindly retrieved our dinghy when, for the second time (and both in Tobormory), I disgraced myself by letting it get adrift. My wife was quite thrilled when her Iona acquaintances arrived, having followed us round Mull. Later we heard that they had continued their adventurous journey north round Ardnamurchan.

When Mary and her friend had been sleeping ashore in a tent there had been peace on board ship at night, but as M.R. was leaving early next morning they spent the night on the floor of the cockpit and we did not have " another quiet night." Our two-day summer now came to an end and rain again " descended in torrents." *Leonora, Jane, Sylvia* (a 1902 " 19/24 " on charter) and *Tinker Bell* (ex *Yeoman*) with the Tennant family on board came into the bay and we all visited each other. With the Tennants was a renowned salvage expert, Capt. D., R.N. When I asked him why he had taken up that speciality he replied quite seriously that it had attracted him because when one was down below there was nobody else there to interfere with one.

The following day we had a short but really good sail. It was blowing fresh to strong from the north-west with heavy squalls and when *Leonora* left for Oban she was heavily reefed. We offered to race *Sylvia* to Loch Aline and she left a quarter of an hour before us also heavily reefed. With one reef down and our storm jib we had all the canvas we wanted and took a lot of water on deck until we bore away at the Green Island. Overtaking *Sylvia* at the entrance to *Loch Aline* we risked a gybe and ran into the loch, having taken only one and three quarter hours for the fourteen miles, eight knots no less, and with no help from the tide.

In the late afternoon my wife who had walked to Ardtornish said that a small yacht beating up the Sound was having a very rough journey. She was the veteran *Golden Plover* with R.A. and B.K. and we soon had them on board for dinner and we all talked till after midnight. Next morning after having lunch with us they left heavily reefed for Tobormory.

The squalls yesterday had been very fierce. My ensign and staff had been blown out of the socket as we lay at anchor ; we luckily found them to-day on the shore about a mile up the loch. At 2 a.m. to the disgust of Mary in the fo'c'sle I veered to thirty fathoms and slipped down an angel as I was not too sure of the holding ground. The " bay " on the west side of the loch just inside the entrance is recommended by the local people and by T. N. Arkle; we must anchor there next time.

The gale lasted another day and night and we then had a pleasant sail to *Puillodobhrain*, speaking *Eala* off Duart Point. As the forecaster now for the first time this cruise spoke of a " high pressure " and a " further outlook of quiet conditions " it may be that we are going to have some fine weather at last, but we doubt it. My wife spent the afternoon sketching ; R.A. had refused to believe that there was not a built fort on Eil. Dun, so she is going to convince him.

A second fine morning ! We got away early for the Garvel-lochs, " The Isles of the Sea " or " The Holy Isles," a row of four isolated, uninhabited, windswept islands lying in the open water between Scarba and Mull, which we had often wanted to visit. On our approach cattle grazing on them, evidently not used to seeing people even in a boat, fled to the other side.

The names of these islands are interesting : Dun Chonail (The Fort of Conall), Garbh Eileach (The Rough Rocky Place), Cuil Bhrianainn (St. Brendan's Retreat) and Eileach an Naoimh (The Holy Rock). It was on the last of these, the most westerly, that we landed. It is almost completely rockbound, but about half-way down the south side there is a small creek, marked on Chart 2326 (Loch Killisport to Cuan Sound) as the " landing place " which is partly sheltered by several rocky islets. My wife and Mary spent some hours ashore but I did not care to leave the ship for long, as although there was little wind the swell was considerable and my anchor seemed to be trundling over a rocky bottom.

There may be some doubt as to whether this is the Hinba to which Columba used to retire for meditation, but it seems certain that a religious community was founded here by St. Brendan, probably before Columba settled in Iona. A few yards from the landing place is a fresh water pool said to have served as a water supply for the settlement. A short distance on one can see the remains of the roofless chapel and a many-chambered building which may have been the monastery. All that remains of these are the dry stone walls. Other ruins in the vicinity may have been underground cells, and some distance away are two well preserved beehive cells. About

LANDING PLACE. See photograph, page 165

200 yards to the south are two upright stones, one with a deeply-cut cross, which are said to mark the grave of Eithene, Columba's mother. If these ruins are the original ecclesiastical buildings of the sixth century they must be the remains of the earliest Christian settlement in Scotland.

When my wife and Mary came on board again I turned down a suggestion that we should go through Coirebhreacain as we would have had to wait for several hours for slack water, so we sailed and then motored down Scarba Sound to Loch Craignish. Before we reached our anchorage at *Ardfern* it was raining again and continued to do so all night.

After two more days of heavy rain I wrote in the log : " The weather is really too atrocious for words ; I think we should sell the boat and the house and emigrate." Yet another gale warning made a passage round " The Mull " inadvisable, so we went into the *Basin, Crinan* and there we stayed for two days while it " rained torrents " and the wireless told us of " intense disturbances," " exceptionally vigorous disturbances " and gales galore. If we hear that down south the Test Match spectators are sitting in their shirt sleeves mopping perspiration from their brows, we will be really cross !

Mameno, ex Rowan III, came in from Charsaig, both owner and wife thoroughly soaked. After a cup of tea with us they moved on to Ardrishaig and then had a very stormy sail to Tarbert. They are certainly making full use of a fine boat.

We were lucky to get through the canal comfortably next day in spite of " an unusually intense disturbance "—I wonder what new descriptions we are going to have of this summer's meteorological conditions—and had a wet sail to *Tarbert*. Leaving there after a night of heavy rain we sailed, again " in torrential rain," through the Kyles of Bute home to Rhu.

At the end of my description of our cruise in 1937 I referred to the extraordinarily bad weather we had had, but this year it was even worse. In this cruise of thirty-seven days we had continuous sunshine on only ten. On only twelve had we light to moderate winds and we specialized in gales, having them on ten of the twelve days on which we had warnings.

But thanks to all the " comforts and conveniences," especially the cockpit cover, we had enjoyed it all. What I may perhaps call the intrusion of Mary and friend rather disturbed the ship's routine and we must take care lest the family again take charge.

III

In Sunshine and Calm

FOR a week after our return my wife and I lived on board at our moorings at Rhu, and, as we had feared, the family and their friends began to invade the ship. After dining Bob, Mary, H.B. and his lady friend, we beat across to *Ardnadam, Holy Loch*, to act as tender to *Gerda*, a *Dragon* owned by Charlie and R.S.

H.B. slept in the cockpit and Mary in the fo'c'sle and when it blew up in the middle of the night and we tailed off too close to a motor boat I disturbed everybody by threatening to lay a kedge. Next day in addition to Mary and H.B. we had on board H.B.'s lady friend, Charlie and R.S., " Dodo," Bob and J.R., and even John turned up from Glasgow. Thank goodness most of them went away before night, but some came back next day for lunch and dinner. This two-berth ship is being used as a boarding house and restaurant !

After two days' racing Charlie and R.S. got away in *Gerda* for a cruise up north and my wife and I returned, in peace at last, to have a few days at Rhu before going off with John to the Baltic, not in *Rowan IV*, but in the Blue Funnel T.S.S. *Ulysses*.

* * *

Cruise Round Mull : August 4th to 18th.—My wife, Neill and myself.

Within an hour of Neill's arrival home on August 4th, from an O.T.C· camp, we got off for a fortnight's cruise with baffles fitted and tanks full. We did not take " Righ " the spaniel with us, as since the tossing we got on our way to Muck he has been scared in anything but very quiet weather.

We met, raced and beat *Redwing* (J.R.C.G.) on our way to *Blackfarland Bay, Bute*, in a light easterly, and had a visit in the evening from *Finora* (M.B.)

Next day we started with a fresh easterly ; after Ardlamont we had a fast run to Ardrishaig and then an easy journey through the canal to *Crinan*. But *Redwing* had beaten us by carrying on round Garroch Head to Ardrishaig the night before, and had, to our regret, locked out a few hours before our arrival. While my wife and I were enjoying a visit from Arnold Gray and his wife, Neill was on board a small cutter which was being sailed single-handed round Scotland.

Leaving Crinan we carried a light easterly and the last of the flood through the Dorus Mor, and after trying unsuccessfully to locate Hutcheson Rock, sailed through the Craobh anchorage and across to *Ardinamir*. This we thought is cruising weather at last, warm and almost too quiet as we had to fall back on the Kelvin for seven hours next day before, creeping gingerly through the Doirlinn Narrows two and a half hours before high water, we anchored at *Tobormory*.

The following morning we left under engine but found a light north-westerly off Runa Gal lighthouse, so being under no obligation to go elsewhere, bore away for the south, and with a little help from the engine got to the south anchorage in Ulva Sound just before high water. Thanks to my recent experience of this enclosed strip of water, which has many charms but few fathoms, we found the correct spot, and were so well sheltered that a fresh south-easterly during the night did not distrub us.

A squall from Ben More as we were leaving next morning gave my wife some anxious moments before we cleared Sgeir Beul, but showed Neill, to his surprise, how handy the old people's boat was under sail. Passing one of the Forth *Dragons* northward bound we ran through Iona Sound and anchored once more in *The Tinker's Hole, Erraid*. A lovely afternoon was spent on the sand in Traigh gheall, where we all bathed, using a weird assortment of garments of my wife's as bathing suits.

Summer had evidently come at last, and with a light easterly we enjoyed a lazy sail past Colonsay to *West Loch Tarbert, Jura*. There was so much mist that we had to rely on our compass before we picked up the north end of Colonsay, and again after losing it until we saw the Jura shore.

Opposite : Ulva Sound (page 138).

I had been told a lot about the difficulties and dangers in navigating this unfrequented loch with its numerous rocks and shoals, but Chart 2481 (Sound of Islay) made it easy. Passing Eil. Gleann Righ on port we kept close to Aird Reambar and then sailed on a line from this point to Rudh 'ant' Sailein ; this cleared Boghachan Baite. As soon as Rudha Gille nan Orlag was abeam we made for the thirteen-feet high islet in the middle of the channel and passed to the south of it. We anchored in the bay west of Cumhann Mor and were lucky not to run on an uncharted reef, which covers at high water, a little to the east of the " 4_2 " sounding in this bay.

There are a great many large caves in this wild uninhabited side of Jura, some of which it is said were used as resting places for the dead on their way for burial in Oronsay or Iona. Martin records that " There is a large cave at Corpich which hath an altar in it," referring to one of those at Corpach Bay, " The Place of Bodies."

When passing down the Jura coast we noticed the extensive raised beaches which at a distance looked like long, flat, grey fields which had been recently limed. On the south side of the loch right up as far as the narrows there is a series of these beaches. It looks as if a gigantic wave had swept in and when receding had left behind it myriads of round grey pebbles.

After we had turned in I heard somebody or something rattling over the shingle, and on looking out saw in the dim light a number of deer close to the edge of the water. As they had not come down for a drink it may be that they were wondering what manner of stranger this was who had invaded their wild lonely home.

For some unaccountable reason even when we find such an unusual and interesting place as this we do not stay to enjoy it, so in order to get the ebb down the Sound of Islay we left early next morning. A cruiser lying overnight off Rudha Mhail conveniently lifted anchor and steamed south just as we were wondering how we ought to salute one of H.M. ships at 7.30 a.m. *Islay* (R.C.C.) the successor of *Widgeon*, was lying near the lifeboat at Port Askaig as we passed, and having evidently seen our burgee, Harvey, followed us into Small Isles, Jura. (Finding no one on board as we were ashore visiting the Nicholsons he sailed out again, but we passed him

next day off Crinan and finally anchored beside him at Tarbert,
Loch Fyne.)

In the afternoon we sailed across the Sound of Jura with a
light northerly and a good deal of mist. With the help of
the compass we picked up Dun Skeig and the entrance to
West Loch Tarbert, Cantyre and ran up to the head of the
loch anchoring behind Eil. Laggan.

The difficulties of navigating this loch have been exaggerated
although the small and irregular rise and fall of the tide necessit-
ate perhaps a little extra care. Chart 2477 (West Loch Tarbert)
shows quite clearly all the rocks and shoals. The foul ground
to the south of Eil. Trein at the entrance, the shoals on its
eastern side and the extensive shoal off Corran Point, can easily
be avoided, but both Ardpatrick House and further up Eil.
Eoin may be a little difficult to pick up.

This was our first visit and we were disappointed. After
the bare, desolate character of its uninhabited namesake in
Jura with its wild life, its clean shores and clear water, this
seemed more like an inland loch with thickly wooded banks,
comfortable houses, and with swans swimming unafraid on
its smooth water. Later when the anchor was lifted clogged
with thick mud from its brackish water, we realized the cleansing
power of tidal streams.

At 4 a.m., hearing heavy rain, in spite of vigorous protests
from my wife, I rose and put up the cockpit cover for which
we were all thankful, as we then had a short but severe thunderstorm with torrential rain.

Next day we had a wet but very invigorating sail with a
strong flood against a fresh north-westerly to *Charsaig, Cantyre*. There was a nasty tide-rip between Corr Eiln. and
Eilean More, and we were tossed about and took a lot of water
on board. On the north side of Eilean More, on which there
are the ruins of a twelfth century chapel, there is a small natural
harbour, but it looked very small indeed. With a reef down
and snoring along we were a little in doubt of our position,
when we suddenly found ourselves off *Charsaig Bay*, and
anchored inside the island just south of Seal Rock.

On our way to the jetty in the dinghy Neill and I were nearly
swamped, and after getting stores at Tayvallich had great
difficulty in rowing back to the ship. The bay itself in north-
westerly winds is very exposed, but although it was blowing

hard in the evening we were comfortable behind the island.

After a quiet sail to *Ardfern*, and a quiet night there, we had no sooner locked in at *Crinan* than the weather showed signs of breaking up, and the glass which had been absolutely steady for ten days began to slip down. We towed *Moyra*, whose engine had broken down, through the Canal next day and then motored in heavy rain to *Tarbert*.

We then had our first gale warning, which was followed next day by a westerly gale. *Moyra* left with reefed mainsail and storm jib and made a record passage to the Gareloch; *Veronica* followed under trysail; *Panther* came in under trysail and a Dragon got into the bay with some difficulty after a very stormy journey from Ardrishaig. My wife went home by steamer; Neill and I foregathered with Harvey and his son, and watched the closing points-race of " The Tarbert Yacht Club " in the harbour. The following day we motored home to Rhu in heavy rain.

Neill, as in our second cruise in 1935, had brought us good weather, so we had rewarded him by showing him some new anchorages. With the exception of the thunderstorm at West Loch Tarbert, Cantyre, we had had continuous sunshine for the first ten days, but the incessant rain on the last three almost made up for this.

IV

1939: To the Outer Hebrides

WITH the idea of making the ship less easily tossed about in rough water the internal ballast was increased by the addition of one ton of lead in moulded blocks. This increased her draft to five feet. The baffles in the water tanks had cured the splashing and there seemed to be nothing else calling for improvement or alteration, although for some reason I still kept the roller reefing gear on the jib in spite of all the annoyance it had given us last year.

* * *

Cruise to Rodel and Gairloch : May 29th to June 27th.—My wife and myself.

Leaving " Righ " again at home we got away in fine weather and had to call on the Kelvin a good deal before we reached Crinan after a night at *Tarbert.* I took advantage of the fresh water in the Basin and the sunshine to wash and varnish the dinghy, and gave it a second coat as it lay on the deck on our way up Scarba Sound next day.

For the second year in succession we missed out Puillodobhrain on our way north, and carrying a light northerly as far as *Loch Aline* turned in there, anchoring just inside the entrance opposite the two white posts on port.

If it is true that no sea comes in here even with a strong south-westerly because of the tidal stream, then it is a better anchorage than the east bay as the holding is better. It is also more conveniently placed for the store, but all my wife was able to get there was a " *Daily Record* and a toothbrush with some difficulty."

We were glad next morning to find a south-easterly, and although the roller jib behaved badly when expected to do the work of a spinnaker, we were soon at *Tobormory. Morweena* (R.C.C.) and *White Cloud* came in later, also the new Fishery Cruiser. *Mat Ali* had been in yesterday so the R.C.C. has been well represented.

In bright sunshine and with very little help from a light south-westerly we motored the following day to *Loch Harport*, anchoring west of *Port na Long* pier. As we were entering the loch we saw a " monster " ; it was white with a small black fin and we thought it was dead and floating upside down, until we noticed that it was moving slowly forward. The people ashore knew of its presence, but could not say what it was. It was certainly neither shark nor seal.

It is time I paid a compliment to this reliable engine which takes us along at six knots in quiet water at three-quarter throttle using only three-quarter gallon of petrol an hour. That it could, if asked, drive us through rough water against a strong head wind was proved several times last year.

The hot calm weather continued and we had a slow reach next day, with the roller jib again behaving badly, to Loch Maddy. When passing Wiay Island we got very close to an enormous number of guillemots which rose from the water and flew away just as I was going to get an unusual photograph.

We had a fine view of MacLeod's Maidens and the cliffs as we took the passage between the Big and Little Mibow. From Neist Point there was very poor visibility, so I set a course, 338 degrees magnetic, but finding that the flood was setting us too far north altered it to 330 degrees. I was stupidly looking for a prominent lighthouse on Weaver Point, and it was some time before I realized that all there was was a small " white hut." Going into the loch by the passage south of Glas More, Fanore Island and the Ree Lee Islets we anchored off the pier in the " South Basin." According to Martin Loch Maddy derives its name from the three Maddies at its entrance, so-called " from the great quantity of big mussels, called Maddies, that grows upon them."

We were not greatly taken with this place ; the anchorage was far too big for our liking and too open, whereas the store was shut. A reply-paid telegram which I sent to Charlie yielding no result after five hours we sailed out again bound for Rodel.

Losing the wind near Harmetry and rolling in a westerly swell, we lowered sail and motored slowly past the Groay Group and found the entrance to *Loch Rodel* very easily by the prominent landmark, St. Clement's Church.

ST. CLEMENT'S CHURCH. See photograph, page 166.

I had read in the R.C.C. Journal of 1911 of the pool or basin on the east side of the loch, but found it difficult to identify the islets enclosing it as they are so like the rough hummocks of the mainland of Harris. So we carried on up the loch and then saw the Ferry jetty and the way in. We tipped the dinghy into the water and my wife rowing in found that there was a least depth of one and a quarter fathoms (it was one and a half hours before high water). Greeting some men on the jetty as we passed I was told where to anchor, and, ever obedient to local instructions, I did as I was told and then found that I was in ten fathoms. Chart 2642 (Sound of Harris) gives no soundings for the pool; the R.C.C. Journal says five or six, but ten was just a trifle too much!

The notes in the West of Scotland *Pilot* on this "small deep-water basin" are not accurate. The entrance from the east is across a rocky barrier which dries; at the inner end of the west entrance there is still a quarter fathom at low water, and the bottom here is sandy and free from obstructions.

After our disappointment at Loch Maddy we were all the more pleased with this, our first anchorage in the Outer Hebrides. The pool is absolutely sheltered, but as the surrounding land is low one has a wide view of the open sea from the east through the south to the west. The *Pilot* is correct in saying that although there may be some swell through the east passage, there is none through the other.

Next day, although it was Sunday, we were able to hire a car and had a most interesting drive over appalling roads up the Sound, past the great stretch of sand "Traigh an Taobh Tuath," up the west coast, across to East Loch Tarbert and back to Rodel. While there is a strange beauty in the barrenness of this rocky country one cannot wonder that its inhabitants find it difficult to get a living out of it. When passing the small post office at the village of Stroud, two miles from Rodel, I got a reply to my telegram and as it brought good news of Mary, then on her way to Australia, the sun seemed to shine all the brighter.

We spent the rest of the day filling up the petrol tanks, showing the ship to the hotel proprietor and looking at St. Clement's Church. This old church, whose tower is said to be the oldest in Scotland, was built in the thirteenth century and restored in 1873. It stands in a splendid position overlooking the loch. Munro says " ane monastery with ane steipell, guhilk was foundit and biggit by M'Cloyd of Harrey, callit Roodill." Inside are a number of old tombs, the principal one being that of Alastair Crotach, the hunchbacked MacLeod, who was responsible for the murder of the MacDonalds at Eigg. It has an effigy of a warrior clad in a complete suit of armour, and on the arch above it are sculptured panels showing an ancient ship, angels and other figures.

We were so courteously received by Mr. McCallum, and so well fed when we dined at the hotel in the evening, that we decided that we must come back here some day and stay for more than a day or two. We both slept badly, probably because we had had too much lobster at dinner, but I was able to lift the anchor and thirty-five fathoms of chain and, pulling the dinghy on deck, we crept out two and a half hours before high water without touching.

We had left early as we wanted to be round Ru Hunish before the three and a half knot westerly tide started, and we were soon snoring along with a fine south-westerly closely followed by a solitary seagull. The only time we had been in these waters before, in 1932 in *Rowan II*, we had been so occupied with navigation that we had not been able to see much of interest on the land. So this time I intended having a good look at Port Erisco, behind Hulm Island, and Duntulm Castle. But having passed Fladdachuain to port and seen Yesker on starboard we found ourselves round Ru Hunish almost before we knew. So all we saw was a ruin high up on the top of a precipitous cliff.

Having seen us safely past Trodday, with an hour to spare, our faithful seagull now deserted us. Finding a southerly, which according to the morning's forecast was to increase, we made for Gairloch. Having taken only seven hours for the forty-five-mile passage, we anchored in one and a quarter fathoms (one hour before low water) in *Badachro*, but later shifted to a spot off a wooden hut on the island opposite the jetty where we got two fathoms. This hunt for sufficient water reminds us of Ulva Sound. " The local people in 1937 put a perch on the "dries twelve-feet" rock ; I must really write to the C.C.C. and point out that it is time they put this rock on their sketch plan."

155

On our way across from Rodel we had noticed a complete solar halo which according to the books is " seen on the edge of a depression," so we were not surprised when next day the glass fell and the southerly increased. We went to Gairloch by the local bus, " a quite magnificent Dodge," with a few other passengers all of whom spoke Gaelic. After visiting M. McI., a friend of Mary's, we walked the long, sweltering miles back, and, like all cruising people who occasionally go ashore, were glad to get back on board again.

Yesterday when nearing the entrance to Gairloch we noticed a cloud of dust in the wake of two cars going along the shore road from Ru Ruag, a most unusual spectacle which showed that there has really been a dry spell. The news that yesterday the shade temperature in Rosshire was ninety degrees and that in the last ten days Glasgow has had 136 hours of sunshine confirms this.

By evening the solar halo had asserted itself and we had heavy rain, the first for two weeks. The following morning also was wet and cold, so we wandered over Horrisdale Island in the forenoon and walked to Port Henderson after lunch. Of quite a number of cottages on the island only one is now inhabited and the pier and " fish factory " are deserted. Port Henderson is a village above a lovely bay looking across the Minch. Between it and the road is an unusual but very courteous notice, " Visitors are respectfully requested not to come through this village on Sabbath."

When we left Badachro on the third morning the tides were not favourable for Ru Re and the outlook " fresh to strong northerly winds " was not encouraging, so we set course for South Rona. Close-hauled with a fresh north-westerly we had a wet sail across until we got shelter from the island, and on opening the Sound of Rona found both tide and wind against us, so stowing sail we motored into *Acarsaid Mor*. This may seem a lazy sort of thing to do, but it is a temptation to which we are not ashamed to succumb. The Raasay-Rona postman, my old patient, was just leaving in his boat as we came in, and after a talk with us left for what would be a rather tricky crossing of the Sound.

This is the fifth time we have been in here ; in 1931 and 1933 with the whole family in *Rowan II*, my wife and myself with " Jack " twice in 1937 and now just our two selves in the old people's boat. We have had changes, but here everything is as it was except that the Macraes are like us, getting older.

In the evening we had our first gale warning, but as this time we were lying well behind the island the strong south-westerly did not disturb us. The warning was repeated in the morning and as it was raining as well as blowing the decision not to move was easily made. The only worry was that we had no bread and only five cigarettes, but there was a plentiful supply of flour. As the cows after calving are allowed to stay " on the hills " we have never been able to get any milk here, but to-day we were told that a cow which calved a few days ago was to be milked, so we are hopeful. (But we were again disappointed.)

The weather seems definitely to have broken and I think it is fortunate that we did not go further north as we have planned to meet *Eala* at Portree in a day or two. We can always jump across from here, but we might have had to wait longer than we wished if we had been north of Ru Re. Workman, of *Morna*, once warned me to treat that headland with great respect and perhaps I have been over-cautious when we were within reach of it and too inclined to find reasons why we should not tackle it. That, at any rate, is my wife's opinion !

We thought of walking up the rough path to the lighthouse three miles away at the north end of the island, but by the time we were ready to start it was blowing so hard that it was not possible to row ashore or rather to row back again. We were sheering about in the gusts that seemed to come from all directions and the chain was constantly grinding against the bob-stay, so I slipped it over the bowsprit crance. In the evening we got ashore for an hour but by the time we got back on board it was blowing as hard as ever and the usual warning followed later.

Next morning after getting yet another warning as the wind was merely fresh, and there was only one cigarette left, we lifted a very muddy anchor and motored to *Portree*. There was a big swell outside and a very confused sea until we were past Fladda, and at the entrance to the bay we got some really fierce squalls, but the Kelvin pushed us through quite easily.

We were disappointed to find no yachts in, but fortunate in getting half a salmon, some stores and of course cigarettes.

We also got a fine batch of letters including a very welcome one from Mary posted at Capetown. We lay at Portree for four days for various reasons; the weather was cold and showery; we wanted to visit some friends; *Eala* had not turned up, but *Judith* (ex *Rowan II*) came in with the owner, an R.A.F. friend and his niece on board.

On one cold afternoon we walked along the Staffin road and inspected the large dun or hill fort whose ruin stands on a hill overlooking the bay. On another day we had a rough journey to Sligachan in an aged bus, with one other passenger and his bicycle, over a road that was being repaired in true Highland fashion. The excellent lobster salad we had at the hotel was worth coming for, but what we enjoyed most was the walk up the glen after lunch.

Our most pleasant visit, however, was to Uig to see an old family friend, the schoolmaster's wife. On the way we passed Kingsburgh where in 1746 Prince Charlie was sheltered for a night after being brought across from South Uist by Flora MacDonald. We had a wonderful view of Uig Bay and the Outer Hebrides from the schoolhouse.

On the fourth day although the glass was still falling the sun came through the mist, so we set off for *Poll Doin* and *Judith* went up Raasay Sound. It was high water when we reached the bay, so we were even more careful than usual. Identifying Airdban we gave it a wide berth to clear Sgeir More (whose beacon has been missing since 1937) and then looked for the beacon on the rock off the south end of Eil. nan Naomb, but this also was away. Seal Rock was, of course, covered, but we picked out the three Ruadh Islets and kept mid-channel. We anchored as far up the bay as we dared go, in three fathoms, with the north end of Rona just open of the west shore. *Judith's* owner had told me of a line—two white posts and a house—which he had found useful when coming in here, but we could find none of them.

We had a long talk with Miss M. at Airdban Farm, and then walked over the hill to Coillegillie. Glass falling steadily; heavy clouds everywhere; wind southerly for which we were thankful as this anchorage would be uncomfortable in northerly winds.

POLL DOIN. See photograph, page 167.

My wife being restless next day wanted " to go places " and would not believe that it was blowing fresh outside. She laughed at my caution in lifting the dinghy on board as we were merely going round to *Plockton*. But after leaving the bay and the shelter of Crowlin More we found a big sea and a westerly that was rapidly increasing from fresh to strong. There were very heavy showers, but luckily it cleared as we got near Dubh-avid and, picking up the " Conspicuous Tower " on Cat Island, took the passage between it and Sgeir Golach, whose perch we could see.

The buoy marking Hawk Rock has been missing for some years, but a line from the one-foot high rock on Sgeir Golach to the highest point of Sgeir Buidhe clears it. The beacon on Bogha Dubh Sgeir is still there, but a rock off Ard Vourar has to be guarded against. This rock is marked on the C.C.C. Journal sketch plan, but not in Chart 2639 (Lochs Carron and Kishorn). The bay shoals far out, but we got one and a half fathoms about half-way between the railway bridge below the Castle and Eil. nan Gamhainn. A red flag on a home-made spar buoy off Cat Island had puzzled us ; it turned out to be a mark for the local regatta which, however, was cancelled as it was blowing too hard.

Although it was a half-holiday and the store and Post Office were shut, I was able, perhaps because I was wearing a jersey, to buy new potatoes, bananas, etc., and to send a telegram to Charlie and a postal order to Neill.

It is true, I believe, that this quiet little village of Plockton was once a busy boat-building and seafaring port, but I fear that Cowper was exaggerating when he wrote, in 1896, that " it actually possesses a Lord Provost and two baron baillies ; while as to tonnage, it owns more vessels than any place from the Clyde to Stornoway."

I ought to have included Plockton in my coastal survey in Part II, as we had spent a night here in *Rowan II* in 1932 on our way from Loch na Beist to Gairloch. We had spent the afternoon behind Kishorn Island and had come into the bay past Sgeir Buidhe and Sgeir Golach. On leaving then, and again this time, we took the south passage which I prefer. If it is clear enough to see the " Conspicuous Tower " there are no difficulties ; if it is thick then both passages are equally difficult.

159

A quiet night; a lovely morning; a walk to Frith-aird and a fine view across to Loch Kishorn to the north and the Skye mountains to the west.

In the afternoon we motored to *Kyle Akin* and entering *The Pool* there did not repeat our 1937 mistake. There was no room for us to anchor so we picked up a mooring, but the picking up was no easy matter as it had an enormously heavy chain. I hauled up just enough to make fast and hoped that the owner would not come in during the night. We got a variety of stores ashore and a huge lobster from a boat just back from the north of Skye.

Between 4 and 5 a.m. I wakened hearing a boat alongside and dashed up on deck in my pyjamas to be told, quite courteously, to go back to bed. It was *Ribhinn 'Og*, whose mooring we had taken, back from Loch Snizort with only seven boxes of herring after a fortnight's fishing. Instead of cursing me they were not in the least annoyed and would not hear of me giving a hand when they shifted that chain to their boat and moored me alongside with their own warps.

We walked over the hill to Loch na Beist next day finding the moor unusually dry but saw no yachts there. *Cutty Sark* came in later and we had a visit from her crew. In the evening there was heavy rain and another gale warning, but we had a peaceful night.

After tidying, sweeping, cleaning and polishing the ship—we seem to do this very often—we had a lazy day reading, having a bath and tea at the hotel, and studying the navigation of Loch Hourn. *Judith* came in from the north and anchored at Kyle of Loch Alsh. They came across after dinner and gave us their news. From Portree they had sailed to Badachro and next day while the Group-Captain and his niece walked to Poolewe the owner and hand had had a wet sail round my bugbear, Ru Re. We discussed all sorts of topics from the usefulness of C.Q.R.'s for flying boats to the prices charged for " chance baths " in hotels. One of them when refusing to pay five shillings for a bath had told the hotel people that it was not the bath itself he wanted, as it was too large for his boat. The joke of the evening was when I asked about that line into Poll Doin which I had not been able to find and we discovered that *Judith* must have been in Poll Creadha when her owner thought they were in Poll Doin.

PLOCKTON and LOCH HOURN. See photographs, page 168.

V

The Loch of Hell

AFTER more visits from the crews of *Cutty Sark* and *Ribhinn 'Og* we left next morning, and joining *Judith* sailed through Kyle Rhea; she carried on for Tobormory, while we bore away into *Loch Hourn*.

Perhaps I have been a little scared of Loch Hourn, like Ru Re, making the excuse of wanting to get north, or having to hurry south when passing it. To-day we had no excuse and were fortunate in having a light westerly when exploring this " Hell Loch " for the first time.

Passing south of the iron beacon on Sgeir Ulibhe we held along the north shore and had a look at Camus Ban behind Eil. Tioram and the little village of Arnisdale lying below the 3196 feet high Ben Sgriol. We then crossed to the south side where at first glance Camus Doin looked an ideal anchorage sheltered as it is by Eil. Mhuinteil. But overlooking it was the even higher Ladhar Bheim and the squalls from this mountain are said to be worse than from Ben Sgriol.

The white sandy shore of Barrisdale with the low-lying green glen behind it seemed almost out of place in this wild loch, but helped to emphasize its magnificent beauty.

Using Chart 2497 (Loch Hourn) we had no difficulty with the first three narrows as all the landmarks are easily identified. At the first we kept south of Coir Island and close to Eil. Garbh-lain. Approaching the second we picked up Cnoc of Kyle, " a low point with a wooded rocky knoll on its inner part," and kept close to the opposite shore, but not too close because of a rock there which covers. Next came the narrows at Eil. Mousker which lies in the fairway and has a shoal off its south-west side, but is steep-to on its south-east side. We kept a little to the north of mid-channel here to avoid the shoal from the south shore.

Following our usual custom we arrived at the fourth narrows at the head of the loch far too early, only one and a half hours after low water, and anchored off Skiary. We then explored the channel which is narrow, winding and shallow—only half fathom at low water. Before I was able to row the dinghy back against the strong flood I had to land my wife. I reported a similar manœuvre at Ulva Sound, so in fairness to my wife I should record that it was due not to her excessive weight, she is only ten and a half stone, but to the strength of wind or tide !

At three hours flood we motored in and anchored off the steps on the north-east side of the land-locked basin. These steps are not shown on the chart; the "steps" below the boathouse on the chart are beside shoal water and would be very inconvenient. In the afternoon we walked round the head of the loch passing through the Lodge garden with its fine collection of eucalyptus trees. In the evening there was heavy rain, and then silence and a sense of desolation. We tried to make friends with a lonely seagull but failed and this seemed to increase the gloom.

It was so peaceful as we had sailed quietly up the loch that it was hard to realize that it often lives up to its evil reputation. The West of Scotland *Pilot*, which is usually guarded in its language, states that " it has about the heaviest rainfall of any loch in the Highlands ; from the great height and close proximity of its surrounding mountains it is a gloomy place when the clouds hang low on their sides." It goes on to warn the sailor that " violent squalls come down off the high land from all directions whipping the surface of the water into a white foam." This description confirmed the tales the Kyle Akin fishermen told me of their experiences there in winter.

Loch Nevis is almost isolated by having no road, but even though this loch is connected with the outside world by the road to Tomdown and Invergarry it is indeed a lonely place of gloomy grandeur. We were glad we had come but were not sorry to leave next morning, two hours before high water.

* * *

We motored as far as Rudh Ard Slisneach before getting a light north-easterly which rapidly increased through moderate to fresh as it so often does in these parts in the early forenoon. Three hours later we were off Eigg and as the roller jib was bothering us we stowed it below and kept the engine " ticking over." Seeing a yacht rolling and pitching off the jetty at

Eigg there was no temptation to put in there, so we carried on managing to get past Eil. Castle still on starboard gybe. Once past Maxwell Bank we gybed and with a fine breeze were soon round Ardnamurchan. We got some heavy squalls from the cliffs before we bore away and ran into *Tobormory*. We had taken just over eight hours for the fifty miles, and from Ru na Fhaochag had averaged well over seven knots.

We picked up one of the Western Isles Yacht Club's moorings beside *Judith*, who had had a long slow beat south yesterday. We then tried to beat each other at rolling ; she gave it up and sought peace at Loch Aline, but we endured it as we were expecting a batch of letters from the family. We woke late next morning and spent the day doing odds and ends including washing down and varnishing the topsides. As no letters had arrived I wired Charlie asking him to send them on. In the afternoon *Ron II*, *Verve* (Wylie) and *Morna* came in and we were on board *Verve* and *Morna* till midnight.

We were all greatly intrigued by the behaviour of a sturdy little cutter which came into the bay under engine and tiny jib. She had been chartered by an elderly gentleman who, on the strength of a very limited experience of sailing, had invited a friend to come cruising with him, and to bring his wife and daughter, none of them having ever been in a yacht before. Having been escorted as far as Brandy Stone by a hand from the yacht yard they had set off on their own up the Sound, and when the wind strengthened, had got into trouble at the Fuenary Rocks. According to the friend they found themselves heading for some rocks and, as they could not think of any other way of avoiding them, had lowered their sails. Having thus escaped from this danger they started their engine and hoisting a jib beat up to Tobormory with this strange combination of sail and power.

As they passed through the Bay the charterer (I will call him the C.P.) asked several yachts about the depth of water, and then ignoring all advice anchored close to the old pier in little more than one fathom at high water. Hands from various yachts when going ashore told him that he would dry out and ought to shift, but he stayed where he was, and having laid a hurricane lamp on the fore deck as a riding light, retired to his bunk.

I looked out at 4 a.m. and saw her high and dry ; they had taken the ground at 2 a.m. and the ladies having got ashore somehow and being wet and cold had spent the rest of the night walking up and down trying to get warm. Looking out again at 6.30 a.m. I saw that she was lifting and when the C.P. was towing her past us later suggested that he should take the mooring next me. To my astonishment he asked me, " what will I do with it ? " so I went across and made his boat fast, but not before the friend had let the winch clutch slip and the anchor down on top of the moorings. We were sorry for the ladies whose first experience of the joys of cruising was rather disconcerting, and my wife did what she could for their comfort.

It was now blowing fresh from the north-east. *Verve* left for Loch Aline under mizzen, jib and engine and *Morna* under reefed main and mizzen for the north. We were most uncomfortable, rolling and pitching, but we were determined to get those letters so just grumbled and bore it. As they had not come by evening I 'phoned Charlie and found that he had forgotten to send them. " Awfully sorry "— quite a family expression this ! We ought to have moved across to Calve Island to get away from the swell, but somehow did not think of it and in spite of the motion slept soundly.

When the owner of *Ron II* told me next morning that he was going to Puillodobhrain I suggested that as the C.P.'s boat was flying the burgee of the C.C.C., of which he was a flag officer, it was up to him to shepherd them down the Sound to that sheltered anchorage. But shirking this responsibility he hoisted sail and made for Oban. Shortly afterwards *Eala* appeared from Drumbuy. She had not been at Portree, but had followed us, a day or two later, into Acarsaid Mor, Badachro and Plockton. When I told them of the plight of the C.P.'s friends, one of their strong crew, Dr. L., volunteered to give them a hand to Puillodobhrain. This offer of assistance was, somewhat reluctantly, accepted by the C.P.

Just before we were leaving we got a warning of a gale, north-west veering north for this region, which rather worried us, but we decided to risk it. Robertson and I agreed that if we found it was too heavy for the C.P.'s boat we could all go into Loch Aline or Loch Spelve. Going out through the Doirlinn Narrows I headed the convoy, *Eala* coming along later at the tail. We had a fast run down the Sound, and still

Top. *Rowan IV* AND HER CABIN. AUTHOR AND HIS DAUGHTER AT TEA
Above. "LANDING PLACE," EILACH AN NAOIMH   8 KNOTS IN THE SOUND OF MULL

ST. CLEMENT'S CHURCH, RODEL, HARRIS

INTERIOR OF ST. CLEMENT'S CHURCH, RODEL, HARRIS

POLL DOIN, INNER SOUND OF RAASAY

ENTRANCE TO LOCH CARRON, SHOWING "THE CONSPICUOUS TOWER"

At Plockton, Loch Carron

Loch Hourn Head

in the lead I showed Dr. L. the way into Puillodobhrain, a new anchorage for him. He ended a graphic description of his experience later with the words " never again ! "

In the afternoon the ladies walked over the hill to Clachan and the experienced ones told the two novices that their troubles were now over as this was an absolutely safe sheltered lagoon.

But we had forgotten about the gale warning ! Late in the evening when my wife and I were on board *Eala* a north-east gale suddenly got up, and as I had selfishly chosen the best spot, off the trap-dyke, I was the only one well sheltered. Through the spindrift we saw the C.P.'s boat dragging right up the bay. The wind was so strong that we could not go to her assistance and it was after midnight before my wife and I were able to get back to our boat only a short distance away.

In a lull during the night Robertson rowed down to see what had happened to them and found that they had picked up just before going ashore. The friend and the two ladies were huddled miserably in the cockpit wondering what was going to happen next in this " sheltered lagoon," but the C.P. was asleep in his bunk in the fo'c'sle. Robertson laid a kedge for them, and next day when shifting them we found that they had dragged because of a foul anchor, a mishap that could not befall either *Eala* or *Rowan IV*. Cruising in the West Coast of Scotland even in what we call summer is not like " sailing on the Norfolk Broads," but as Shakespeare wrote, " Fortune brings in some boats that are not steered."

After that disturbed night we had a quiet day and did not make use of a fine fresh northerly, but preferred to walk and talk, or merely to talk. With a moderate northerly we sailed the following day to *Ardfern* with *Eala* and to our surprise and gratification had no difficulty in keeping ahead of her.

I had hoped to show my wife the way home round " The Mull," but the light breeze that took us out of Loch Craignish soon faded away, and not caring to motor all the way to Gigha we turned back and locked in at *Crinan*. *Fearnought* (R.C.C.) who turned back for the same reason, came in later and we enjoyed their company.

We consoled ourselves for this disappointment by leaving the yacht there and returning to Rhu by steamer, so that

Charlie might be well on his way when he started on his short cruise in August.

The weather had been much better this year ; we had enjoyed every minute of the exceptionally fine spell at the beginning of our cruise and had not grumbled too much at the variety of conditions we had experienced on our way south from Gairloch. That had again been our farthest north as Ru Re had again beaten me, but we counted ourselves lucky in having had quiet weather for our visit to Rodel and Loch Hourn. We were glad to have renewed our friendship with the kindly folk at Kyle Akin and had seen a lot of our old cruising friends.

During the next month we came back by car several times for the week-end bringing "Righ" with us. He had not, however, forgotten his unpleasant experiences, and even in the quietness of the Basin was unwilling to come on board although he had no hesitation in visiting any other boat there without invitation.

To round off our cruising this year we had two days in Loch Craignish, and having at long last scrapped the roller reefing gear on the jib, which now hanked to the forestay, wondered why we had delayed so long.

* * *

Charlie's Cruise to Gairloch with Neill and R.S.:

As usual they kept no log but reported on their return that they had been at Tobormory, Isle Ornsay, Plockton, Badachro, Portree, Scalpay, Inverie, Tobormory, The Bull Hole, Easdale, Loch na Keal, Crinan and Tarbert.

They were lucky in their weather, having south-westerly winds going north and northerlies home from Kyle (where a second R.S. joined them.)

They seem to have behaved well as there was no evidence of torn sails, broken planks or dents in the keel. I do not know where the fourth member of the crew slept, in the cockpit or on the cabin floor, but after the cramped quarters four of them had when cruising in *Rowan III* they found they had plenty of room.

It seemed inevitable, if not quite correct, that two of the 1934 mutineers should be in charge on the last cruise of *Rowan IV* before the war put an end—for the time being—to cruising, but youth *will* be served.

170

Epilogue

Conclusions on Family Cruising

AFTER twelve years cruising with my family I am, I venture to think, entitled to draw some conclusions about the kind of equipment they should have in combat with the elements.

Just as it takes all sorts of folk to make up the world, so there are all manner of ships on the sea. The type of yacht best suited for cruising depends on various, often conflicting conditions, the cruising ground, the crew, the time available, and is in the end a compromise.

Draft.—In the West Coast of Scotland as we have plenty of water below as well as above, there is no need to restrict the draft. Provided an intelligent use is made of charts and lead, there is no reason for not remaining afloat in spite of all our rocks and tidal streams.

Accommodation.—There should be berths for all the crew. It may be difficult to find sleeping quarters ashore and there are inconveniences associated with a tent. It is pleasant indeed to crawl out of a small tent on a lovely sunny morning and step on the dry springy grass, but in wet weather the reverse is the case. And what a cool reception awaits the man who comes back on board carrying a wet sodden mass of canvas and asks where he is to stow it !

In *Rowan I* the family had their preliminary training in how to live on a boat, and being a bit cramped for space we all got our sharp corners smoothed off. The arrangements in *Rowan II* were almost perfect until some of the crew got too big for their berths. For able-bodied lads—should not one nowadays include the lassies—nothing could be better than a converted six-metre. Two or three could cruise for months on end in *Rowan III* without quarrelling, but I think that in dirty weather four was one too many. But when the joints begin to creak and the muscles are less supple, in other words when one is getting old, some more comfort is desirable. In *Rowan IV* my wife and I had a boat in which, but for Hitler, we could have cruised extensively for many years in safety, without undue exertion and, no matter what the weather was, in comfort.

Rig.—We found the mizzen in *Rowan II* of little use on the wind. Unless this sail is well inboard it has little driving power, so under about fifteen tons have only one mast.

With children on board Bermudian rig is undoubtedly safer, and of course very easy to handle, but the tall mast is a disadvantage. For cruising the old-fashioned gaff mainsail is better. If you have roller reefing have the ordinary reefing gear as well and have a second topping lift as an additional safety measure. Have the jib hanked on to the forestay ; I do not know why I put up with roller reefing on the jib for so long ; it is a very clever but often most annoying contraption.

Auxiliary.—Even in a six-metre, which ghosts along in the lightest of airs, an auxiliary is an advantage if you must be home when you ought to be. No matter how cleverly an out-board engine may be fitted it is useless if there is any swell, so have a small engine installed inboard. Some of our headlands are very exposed and sudden changes of weather frequent even in summer and if your boat has not good windward qualities you may have to depend on power. If this is to push you through against a strong headwind and sea be sure you have enough of it.

Personally I am quite happy with petrol ; it is clean, and if proper precautions are taken it is safe. Interrupted filling pipes will keep water out of the tanks ; accessible turn-off cocks and a second fire extinguisher away from the engine will allow you to tackle a fire without delay. A water-jacketted exhaust pipe or silencer is the only reliable way of preventing water getting back into the cylinders.

Ground Tackle.—The 72-lb. Fisherman we had on *Rowan II* had splendid holding qualities, but there was always the risk of its being fouled no matter how carefully laid. With the C.Q.R. of half its weight we had nothing but satisfaction except on one occasion when, before I had got accustomed to handling it, it tried to nip off one of my fingers. An angel of about 26 lbs. slipped a few fathoms down the chain is useful in checking snubbing or when there is little swinging room. A kedge may occasionally be necessary, and it is an advantage to have a couple of fathoms of, say, ⅜-in. chain between it and the coir warp.

The double-acting lever winch in *Rowan II* was good, but the mast-winch in *Rowan IV* was much better. With the chain carried over the bowsprit crance one can with a minimum of exertion sail away with the shank of the C.Q.R. lashed to the bowsprit. This fully justified the presence of a rather unsightly short bowsprit.

The chain locker should be directly below the fairlead, and if it is divided vertically the chain is not only self-stowing, but comes out without fouling. The grating at the foot of the locker, by allowing it to be washed out frequently, saves one the trouble of getting all the mud off the chain at the inconvenient time of lifting anchor.

Dinghy.—When the children were on board I preferred to tow the dinghy in case one of them fell overboard, but I am justly proud of the fact that I was the only one who did this. With the painter shackled to the stem at the waterline we had no trouble when running, but the dinghy was literally a drawback when on the wind. On the occasion, at the end of our two months' cruise in *Rowan III*, when it filled and sank, this shackle was not being used.

We were able in *Rowan IV* to have the eight-feet dinghy on deck, where it ought to be. It stowed so securely over the skylight that it was not lashed down, and could be slipped into the water in a minute or two. I had arranged to hoist it on board with a wire span and the peak halyards, but found that this gear was unnecessary as one person could easily haul it on board.

Cockpit Cover.—If one is to keep dry below—and this is very necessary—a well-fitting cockpit cover is essential. It may be supported by stanchions or simply over the boom, but it must be easily removable.

Charts.—I shocked many of my friends by cutting up all my charts into sections of about eleven inches by fourteen inches and backing them. The slight error in laying off a bearing was more than compensated for by the convenience of having a chart in a celluloid case in one's hand in the cockpit. At Acarsaid Mor when we took the wrong side of Rough Island the handiness of the chart undoubtedly saved an awkward situation, and there were many other occasions when it was a great advantage, for example, when finding our way into the Gigha anchorage in a deluge of rain.

I was often blamed, in fact jeered at, for my caution, but my good fortune in not hitting any rocks or taking the ground in our twelve years' wanderings was chiefly due to the constant use of the chart, not below but in the cockpit.

Cooking.—A good cook with a poor stove can have fair success with much trouble, but a poor cook can make a mess of things no matter what facilities she, or he, has. In a small boat, like *Rowan I* or *III,* one has to be content with Primus stoves, which are difficult to keep clean, prone to leak, and impossible to regulate. (It is wise to carry spare nipples and washers as well as a plentiful supply of prickers.) The Latham in *Rowan II* was an improvement, but it was only when we had the Calor gas stove in *Rowan IV* that my excellent cook got the instrument she deserved. There will probably be after the war all sorts of new devices which will replace the Primus, but the Calor will take some shifting.

Water.—Not only for cooking but for washing, both domestic and personal, one should carry as much water as possible. Have as large a tank, or tanks, as you can fit in, but be sure to have baffles fitted. If you have not room for a tank a couple of three-gallon tins will suffice, but on no account have a " breaker " so-called because it breaks both your back and your temper. We had one in *Rowan I,* but never again.

Food.—We carried a large stock of tinned food, but nearly always managed to get fresh vegetables, meat, milk and fruit. If bread was short, and my wife was on board, freshly baked scones appeared as if by magic. The meat safe we had in *Rowan IV* was a great improvement on the usual deck type. Efficiently ventilated from outside, its position and accessibility saved my wife in the galley many a wet journey.

Wireless.—Our early sets were unreliable, but a two-valve " Sloop " in *Rowan III* and a three-valve " Schooner " in *Rowan IV* gave us good service. The keel was used as an

" earth " and the shrouds as " aerial," no special insulation being employed.

I relied perhaps too much on weather forecasts and paid too much attention to gale warnings, but there were many occasions when they saved us a lot of trouble.

Books.—We always carried a lot of books on board, although we seemed to have little time for reading. The list includes the C.C.C. Journal, the West of Scotland *Pilot* (more useful for ships than yachts), the *Manual of Seamanship*, Vol. I, Claud Worth's *Yacht Cruising, The Log of the Blue Dragon,* and, with apologies to Lynam, *Cowper's Sailing Tours,* Part 5. *Skeletta* and *Para Handy* refused to be left ashore, although some of the family knew them " off by heart." There were many others including books on the flora and fauna of Scotland and a *Pear's Annual,* which settled many disputes.

To satisfy my wife's keen interest in things of the past we had with us Childe's *Prehistory of Scotland,* Andersons' *Scotland in Pagan Times,* and *The Stones of Scotland* by Scott-Moncrieff.

Dr. Johnson's Journey to the Western Islands of Scotland and *Boswell's Tour of the Hebrides with Dr. Johnson* were, of course, on board, and were often referred to. Only recently I have come across the book which may have been the reason for Johnson's journey. It is " *A Description of the Western Isles of Scotland,* circa 1695, by Martin Martin, Gent."

In a copy of the first edition (1703) of this book in the National Library, Edinburgh, is the following note in Boswell's handwriting : " This very book accompanied Mr. Samuel Johnson and me in our tour to the Hebrides in April 1773. Mr. Johnstone told me that he had read Martin when he was very young. Martin was a native of Skye, where a number of his relatives still remain. His book is a very imperfect performance, and he is erroneous as to many particulars, even some concerning his own island. Yet as it is the only book upon the subject it is very well known. I have seen a second edition of it. I cannot but have kindness for him, notwithstanding his defects. James Boswell, 16th August, 1774."

It seems probable that it was the reading of this book that induced Johnson to visit the Hebrides although he criticized it with his usual frankness :—" no man now writes so ill as Martin's account of the Hebrides is written."

A much earlier description of the Western Islands was written by Sir Donald Munro, " High Dean of the Isles," after a personal visit in 1549. It was, however, not published till 1774, when only fifty copies were printed. A reprint of this, in its original form with the curious old spelling and names, is included in the 1934 edition of Martin's book.

Dogs.—In many ways a dog in a small yacht is a nuisance ; on coming on board after a run ashore, which may include a visit to a farm, he usually parades up and down a newly-scrubbed deck ; he must be taken ashore morning and evening no matter what the weather is like ; he is apt to disappear just when we are ready to move off, and he seems to think the best corner in which to sleep when we are sailing is on a coil of main or jib sheets.

But what a good companion he is, and what a difference he made to the enjoyment of the family in their rambles ashore.

Even on our occasional long passages our dogs did not seem to suffer any inconvenience, but if, as in the case of " Righ " the spaniel, they get scared it is kinder to leave them ashore.

Tidiness.—In a small boat there is no doubt that " cleanliness is indeed next to Godliness," but tidiness is even more necessary. This was the order of the day and my wife saw that it was strictly enforced.

* * *

I did not preface this bundle of log leaves by a formal dedication as I thought it did not merit that honour. But to the reader who has not tired of turning over these pages let me now say that the experiences they record would never have taken place but for the candid criticism, the eager encouragement and the staunch support of the best Mate afloat—my wife.

> *Like leaves on trees the race of man is found,*
> *Now green in youth, now withering on the ground ;*
> *Another race the following spring supplies,*
> *They fall successive, and successive rise.*

INDEX

INDEX

INDEX

181

ROBERT ROSS YACHTING BOOKS

SAILING DAYS By K. ADLARD COLES

" This very attractive book is like a gleam of sunshine on a dull day. . . . The practised pen of the author imparts life to Channel cruising and to races such as that ' Round the Island,' while the very excellent photographs recall vividly the old haunts. . . ."—Sir Alker Tripp in *Yachting Monthly*. **Profusely Illustrated.   8/6 net.**

CRUISING YACHTS :
DESIGN AND PERFORMANCE
By T. HARRISON BUTLER, A.I.N.A.

This book covers the whole subject of yacht designing, including the theory of hull balance, from the first rough sketch to the completed drawing and specification. Into it is woven much practical knowledge of little ships and the details which contribute to comfort and seaworthiness.

With fifty-one line drawings and complete plans of some of the author's most successful designs.   **15/- net.**

LET'S GO CRUISING
By ERIC C. HISCOCK

In this book Mr. Hiscock, Associate Editor of *The Yachtsman*, writes in a light and entertaining manner about the practical side of cruising ; the different yachts, the advantages and disadvantages of their rigs, gear and fittings ; of seamanship and heavy weather ; of pilotage, navigation and cruising grounds.

With more than fifty half-tone illustrations and thirteen line drawings.   **9/6 net.**

TO BE PUBLISHED SHORTLY:

SOUTH and EAST By HENRY ROOKE

A particularly readable account of sailing experiences aboard a converted trawler in all sorts of weather, and ocean racing in a yacht across the North Sea.

TRIM LITTLE CRAFT Some Hints on
Keeping Her that Way. By TERENCE L. STOCKEN.

Explains in simple language how a small yacht can be fitted out and maintained by the amateur in a trim and seamanlike manner. With seventeen line drawings.

Publishers :
ROBERT ROSS & CO., LTD.
ROLLS HOUSE, 2, BREAMS BUILDINGS, LONDON, E.C.4

TRENCH HOUSE
REFERENCE
LIBRARY

St. Joseph's College of Education,

WITHDRAWN

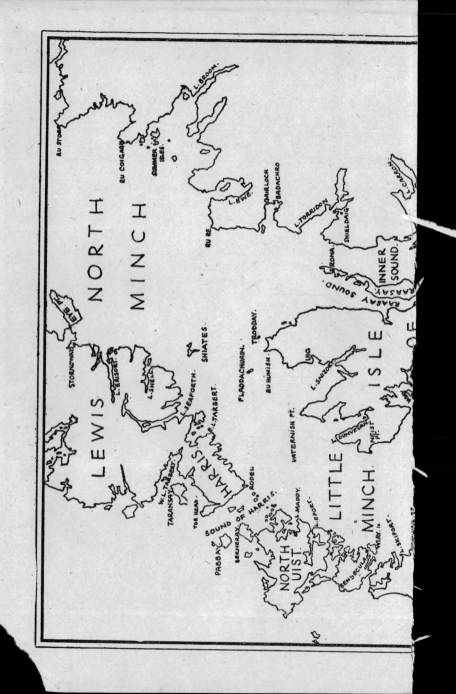

LEAVES
FROM
ROWAN'S
LOGS

TRENCH HOUSE
REFERENCE
LIBRARY